Offering the Gospel to Children

FORWARD BY JOHN WESTERHOFF

# Offering the Gospel to Children

Gretchen Wolff Pritchard

COWLEY PUBLICATIONS
Cambridge ◆ Boston
Massachusetts

Published in the United States of America by Cowley Publications, a division of the Society of St. John the Evangelist. No portion of this book may be reproduced, stored in or introduced into a retrieval system, or transmitted, in any form or by any means—including photocopying—without the prior written permission of Cowley Publications, except in the case of brief quotations embodied in critical articles and reviews.

International Standard Book Number: 1-56101-065-0
Library of Congress Number: 92-23900

Cover Illustration, *Dorelia with Three Children*, by Augustus John, reprinted with permission from Mrs. Vivian White in London.

Library of Congress Cataloging-in-Publication Data
Pritchard, Gretchen Wolff.
Offering the gospel to children / Gretchen Wolff Pritchard ;
foreword by John Westerhoff.
p. cm.
Includes bibliographical references.
1. ISBN 1-56101-065-0 (alk. paper)
BV1475.2.P75   1992
268'.432—cd20                    92-23900

This book is printed on recycled, acid-free paper and was produced in the United States of America.

*Fourth printing*

Cowley Publications
28 Temple Place
Boston, Massachusetts 02111

*For Arnie*

# Acknowledgments

THIS BOOK BRINGS together a variety of essays, sermons, and other pieces with a common theme, written (and often re-written) over a period of almost ten years. The influence and the love of many people are reflected in it.

The earliest of these chapters were written, and many others were conceived and began to grow, when the Rev. Beth McLaren asked me to write her my thoughts on infant communion soon after the birth of her son, and later invited me to lead a series of adult classes. The Parish Development course offered in the Diocese of Connecticut gave me much-needed tools for insight into the joys and frustrations of the ministry of parish education. The clergy of St. Paul's, New Haven, have been my friends and colleagues for thirteen years and have generously allowed me to preach on many occasions.

More than half these chapters originally appeared in my column "All God's Children" in *The Living Church*. I am grateful to the Rev. H. Boone Porter for inviting me to write them and for allowing their incorporation into this book.

In workshops and conferences where I have been asked to speak, I have received many ideas and insights, much loving support, and much help in clarifying and presenting my own thoughts. Special thanks are due to Betsy Rodnok and the people of the Diocese of Texas, who served as audience for much of the material in this book as it was taking its final form.

This book belongs especially to the children of St. Paul's, who have given me more than I will ever give them, and to the many friends and colleagues who have worked with me, inspired me by their love of children, listened to my ideas, and freely offered their own, especially Jack and Sherry Ellis, Lee Howard, Myra and Don Ferree, Tom Pellaton, Susan Amussen, Jodi Mikalachki, Lori Hanna, Christen Frothingham, Klara Tammany, Ellen Davis, Dwayne Huebner, Liz Cox, Joanne Neel-Richard, Chip Chillington, and Jim Thrall. Most of all, this book belongs to my family— to Arnie, and to our children, Grace, Margaret, and Marion, for whom we have the fearsome responsibility not only of offering the gospel but of trying to live it.

# Table of Contents

# FOREWORD

## by JOHN H. WESTERHOFF

ONLY ON RARE occasions do I accept an invitation to write the introduction to a book. When I do, it is because I believe the book to be significant and deserving of recognition; I wish I had written it myself and am honored to be connected with it; and since I am enthusiastic about its contents, I think I might have a few things to add that would reinforce its message.

Such is the case with Gretchen Wolff Pritchard's *Offering the Gospel to Children*. Of course I have known and admired her work for many years; indeed, I consider us to be kindred spirits. While I have no reason to believe she has read or been influenced by my own work, I can easily identify harmonious theological, liturgical, and educational convictions and commitments.

Over a decade ago I wrote *Bringing Up Children in the Christian Faith*. There, after defending the idea of being with children rather than doing things to or for them, I made four recommendations: that we tell and retell God's story as found in the Scriptures until it becomes our common personal story; that we participate in liturgy and share eucharist together; that we listen to and talk to each other about our experiences and relationship with God; and that we practice performing faithful acts of ministry together.

While I was writing about faithful ways of being with children, however, Gretchen Pritchard was doing them—all the while recording her experiences and creating imaginative resources to help others do the same. For this I was delighted, though a bit envious.

Recently our paths crossed for the first time because we were in an educational program together, and I took the opportunity to participate in her workshop. I told her of my enthusiasm for her imaginative designs for being with children and transmitting the church's story through liturgy and learning. I also encouraged her to put her experiences, convictions, and insights into some form that would make them available to the church, for we needed them very much. It was not many months later that I received her editor's request to read and write an introduction to this book.

*Offering the Gospel to Children* is in the best sense a story book that not only speaks of the power and purpose of story, but is also an incarnation of that purpose and power. Gretchen Pritchard is an artist who understands the deepest implications of learning with children. By inviting her readers into her life experience with honesty, humility, and humor, she reveals to us the hidden dimensions of being faithful with children in our day. By doing so, she has given new life to our understanding of worship with children, provided us with new possibilities for the church school, offered a new vision for foundational parish education, and suggested new insights into Christian formation. Very simply, this is a book for which many of us in Christian education have been waiting.

After I finished reading her book for the second time, a number of thoughts surfaced. First I recalled a seminal book by George Steiner, *Real Presence*, in which he makes a telling criticism of the state of the arts in our day. Instead of nurturing a society of poets and writers, composers and musicians, painters and sculptors, choreographers and dancers to engage and illuminate us, we have instead a society of critics, commentators, and interpreters to tell us about the arts, both their value and their meaning. By so doing, Steiner contends, we have denied ourselves any personal involvement with the arts and prevented them from influencing our lives; instead, we have permitted our minds to be shaped by those who write about them.

It strikes me that we have a similar phenomenon in the church. Rather than encouraging ourselves and our children to enter the biblical story through the arts, we have told our children about someone else's moral or theological interpretation. Rather than participating in the whole story in its most original and unedited form, we have shared small pieces of the story that we consider appropriate for children at various ages—again, mainly for the purpose of communicating someone else's understanding of the story's meaning.

Gretchen Pritchard wisely wants to change that situation. Here she not only explains why, but how. Other artists have shared her convictions, Madeleine L'Engle, for one. In *Walking on Water* L'Engle comments on well-intentioned adults who do not want their children polluted by fairy tales, fantasy, and myths, thereby not only denying them their childhood, with all its imagination and creativity, but also their chance to enter into the sacred world of revealed truth—truth that goes deeper than laboratory proofs. As a child she knew intuitively that Hans Christian Anderson's fairy tales and the Bible stories of Joseph and Jonah belonged to the same world, for the world of the Bible is the world of Story, and story that can speak to us as the very word of God. L'Engle was allowed to read her Bible with the same wonder and joy with which she read the *Ice Princess* or *The Tempest*, and she reminds us that people are sometimes kept from reading the Bible by what they have been taught about it.

In *The Original Vision: A Study of the Religious Experience of Childhood*, the English sculptor, educator, and philosopher Edward Robinson shows that religious experience occurs in advance of cognitive, intellectual ways of thinking and knowing. Through the intuitive ways of thinking and knowing available to children as they participate in nature, the arts, and ritual, children enter the sacred dimension of life and experience the divine. Intellectually mature adults, Robinson suggests, need to become childlike if they are to know and live in relationship with God.

More recently, in *The Language of Mystery*, Robinson focuses on the creative imagination, arguing that imagination and faith are similar in giving "substance to our hopes and reality to the unseen." In a chapter called "Theology and Childhood," he expresses his disappointment with contemporary educational philosophy's obsession with developmental theory. To use the stages of cognitive growth as the framework for educational curricula is to turn everything—the natural world, the arts, even human beings—into objects to be understood, mastered, and manipulated rather than mysterious subjects to be honored and engaged.

This is, of course, what happens when we turn the Bible into an object of investigation but neglect it as a subject that will engage and transform us. There is a great difference between being "childish" and "childlike." To speak of being childlike is to speak of the spiritual potential in each of us that so much of contemporary Christian education ignores, thus allowing the childlike qualities in all of us to become stunted and even to atrophy. *Offering the Gospel to Children* is a testimony to the truth of Robinson's words, but, more importantly, it provides us with a viable alternative.

One final book that is foundational to Gretchen Pritchard's important work is George Lindbeck's *The Nature of Doctrine*, in which he contends that there have been three theories of religion and doctrine. One stresses the cognitive aspect of religion and the ways in which doctrines function as truth—claims to which we are to give intellectual assent. A second emphasizes religion's experiential side and the ways Christians attend to inner feelings and attitudes as the basis for arriving at individual personal meaning, while a third approach attempts to combine the first two. Lindbeck offers an alternative approach in which religion structures human experience and understanding of self and world through myths and sacred narratives that are highly ritualized.

This alternative model is particularly significant when we become aware that contemporary Christian education has tended to neglect the foundations of religious life. For many years we emphasized beliefs as propositional truths to be accepted, but neglected faith. In ethics, we have emphasized moral issues and moral decision-making, but ignored character. And we have attempted to provide significant individual experiences but neglected consciousness, that intuitive awareness that makes particular experiences possible.

We have thus turned to instructional models of Christian education appropriate to those ends and ignored the formational models necessary for fashioning faith, character, and consciousness. For example, we have not helped people to develop an intimate, imaginative, and vivid familiarity with the world of biblical narrative, and so have made it impossible for them to experience the whole of life in religious terms. By neglecting the centrality of ritual worship and keeping children away from "adult" liturgy, or not permitting them full participation, we have made it extremely difficult for their lives to be shaped in Christ-like ways.

Gretchen Pritchard understands that symbols, myths, and rituals are crucial to Christian education. Furthermore, she has integrated in an imaginative way Lindbeck's alternative religious model and my own model of Christian formation.

That brings to a close my introduction and my enthusiastic recommendation of this book, but first let me remind you of the opening words of the First Letter of John: "We declare to you what was from the beginning, what we have heard, what we have seen with our eyes, what we have looked at and touched with our hands, concerning the word of life...that you might have fellowship with us" (1 John 1:3). The "we" in John's letter are the teachers within the Johannine community. It was their role to preserve the story—the tradition—a story they had internalized that they might be in union with Christ and with each other. This is the primary responsibility of the church's teachers. *Offering the Gospel to Children* can provide the stimulus and the help to do just that with our children. Read on!

John H. Westerhoff
The Divinity School
Duke University

Margaret Pritchard

❧

*Christian education is not the communication of correct views about what the various works and words of Jesus might mean; rather it is the stocking of the imagination with the icons of those works and words themselves. It is most successfully accomplished, therefore, not by catechisms that purport to produce understanding, but by stories that hang the icons, understood or not, on the walls of the mind.*

Robert Farrar Capon
*The Parables of Grace*

# Let The Children Come To Me

TEN YEARS AGO, WHEN our family bought its first house, I finally had the opportunity I had been waiting for all my life: the chance to take an undistinguished backyard and turn it into a garden. We had the property fenced; we dug, manured, and fertilized; we planted dwarf fruit trees, dogwoods, rhododendrons, azaleas, roses, vegetables, and flowers. By our last summer there, the climbing rose was up to the second story of the house and the small remaining patch of lawn was surrounded on all sides by a waist-high tangle of flowers, foliage, vegetables...and weeds. The little grass paths I had edged with brick between the raised beds almost disappeared, as the peach tree sagged to the ground under its weight of fruit, the tomato plants overflowed their cages, and marigolds, strawberries, sweet alyssum, and chrysanthemums spilled out over the brick. The garden was much too crowded and not everything thrived, and I didn't care for it as well as I should have...but it was a beautiful place, a magical place.

We moved to that house the same year that Margaret, our second daughter, was born. She was too young to remember how dull and barren the yard was at first; for her it was simply a place of delight. When she was five she told me it was like the Garden of Eden; a year later, when nearly all her play was about princesses, unicorns, and dragons, she said, "Mommy, your garden is so beautiful, it's like a royal pleasure garden."

Several years ago, we sold our house to the owner of the bar and restaurant next door, who had often commented on how nice the garden was and how it enhanced the setting of his business. As soon as we had moved out, he took down the fence and the line of trees separating the two properties, bulldozed the garden, and paved it over for a parking lot.

We have a new house now, with a new and bigger garden, and a huge, beneficent maple tree for the children to climb and swing from. Here, for the first time, we have had room to grow corn and raspberries, and time and work are slowly turning the once patchy lawn and scruffy shrubs into another pleasure garden, filled with flowers and vegetables and fruit trees, and with magic and pretend games and the memories of long summer afternoons and twilit evenings. And, this summer, a new blessing rests on the garden. Under the Rose of Sharon tree, in a rattan basket, our new baby is sleeping: Marion, born on Maundy Thursday, brings healing and joy after three miscarriages and the death of a beloved grandfather.

But we still avoid driving past our old house on Willow Street. And eventually all our daughters, even the baby, will grow up and leave home; no paradise that I can make for them will hold them for long. The most I can hope for is that the memories of their childhood's gardens will remain within them, growing greener and sunnier with the passing years.

The Bible begins in a garden, the paradise garden of the human race's innocence; like the memory of our childhood gardens, the memory of Eden has stayed with us throughout our long history. The story tells us that the world itself is a work of art, made by a consummate artist who is extravagantly in love with his own work; that we, made in the image of that Artist, are made to love that work, honor and keep it. God's intention seems to have been that we should grow up sheltered in the safety of the garden. We would take on more and more of the work of shaping the world, and the much more delicate work of forming bonds with each other—naming each other, "bone of my bones and flesh of my flesh." We would offer our work to God, and God would be pleased. Having given us mastery over the works of his hands, he would crown us with glory and honor.

But something went wrong. The man and the woman turned away from the trust God asked of them, and the garden is no longer theirs, or ours. Cast out into a hostile wilderness to seek their fortune, they begin to act out the long drama of alienation, pain, and fear of death that is the story of us all. The Bible tells a story of exile, of homesickness—of an aching loss that cries out for healing, of a stubborn refusal to be reconciled to our exile, a desperate longing to find again the homeland we have lost. That homeland has many names in the Bible; beginning as a remembered garden, it grows to become a promised city. The lost Eden becomes the promised land and then the holy city of Jerusalem. Over and over again, God's people seem to have come home, only to be driven out once more into pilgrimage, exile, and pain. In their exile the memory grows more ravishingly beautiful year by year, until it becomes a vision of a new heaven and a new earth, where all tears are wiped away.

Our alienation from our Creator and our true selves is what the church calls the Fall, and the church has claimed that it affects the natural order as well: the whole creation, lovely as it is, is prey to futility, waste, and pain, and groans together in travail as it awaits the revelation of God's healing love.

We see the cost of this alienation in our own lives and in the lives of others: friends and neighbors, and distant strangers whose private anguish fills our television screens night after night. The world's pain is unbearable; much of the time, we simply close our eyes and look away. We try to shield ourselves from it—and we try very hard to shield our children. Often we deny it outright—we pretend the creation is still God's garden and our playground. We bring our children to church and cheerlead them through happy hymns about the beauty and goodness of God's world, as if they had never heard of tornadoes or earthquakes, acid rain or bombs; as if they themselves hadn't lain awake last night, worrying, because Mommy and Daddy had another fight and maybe they will get divorced.

We carve up the Bible into "Bible stories," so that few children even suspect that the story of God's people—our story—is not a collection of object lessons or heartwarming anecdotes, but a long story of unbearable loss—and unbearable hope.

And the climax of that story, the pivot on which it all turns, is that however costly our exile is to us, it is infinitely more costly to God, who has chosen not to leave us but to be with us. Like the faithful servant in the fairy tale who could not stop the king's son from opening the forbidden room in the palace, God was unable to hold us in the safety of the garden. And like that faithful servant, he follows us into our exile, stays by us through the trials and anguish that our own folly brings upon us, and, finally, dies for us so that we can marry the princess.

The cross is a mystery and a terror; we feel we would gladly shield our children from it. But I have found that children do not want to be shielded from the cross. Stumbling block and folly though it may be to grown-ups, to children the cross is the power and wisdom of God. Children know that the world is full of terror, that no answers are easy, that no comfort comes without cost, pain, and mystery. It is not the cross that terrifies children, but the false gospel that bypasses the cross and leaves us forever alone with our pain and guilt, and the false gospel of optimism that tries to assure us that Adam and Eve are still in the garden among their tame animals, and there is nothing outside.

*Let the children come to me,* says Jesus; *for to such belongs the kingdom of God. Truly I say to you, whoever does not receive the kingdom of God like a child shall not enter it.*

Why do children love fairy tales and adventure stories? Because these stories portray the world as they know it to be. The world is a place where we are haunted by memories of a time long ago, before the good queen died and the stepmother came, before the princess was driven out of the palace and made to wear rags, when our life was green and golden and safe. The world is a place where we are hurled out of that safety to seek our fortune, or to accomplish a task of overwhelming difficulty and danger; a place where the rules seem arbitrary and adult wisdom leads only to disaster. In such a world, the fairy tales go on to say, a small choice for good or evil may mean life or death, and the despised and deformed prove to be beautiful and of royal blood. It is a place where out of suffering comes new life, not by enlightened application of effort, where we regain our lost paradise not by desperately clinging to it, but by loving all and risking all, by our willingness to accept help from friends we never dreamed of, but who have been beside us all along.

It is the youngest son who always inherits the kingdom: the one who admits he is young and foolish and does not pretend to know all the answers. Entering the kingdom as a little child means we encounter the Bible not as a source of rules and formulas, but as a story—and it is a story about us. We are far from home in a world is full of terror, and we cannot help ourselves, but neither can we give up our vision and be reconciled to things as they are.

But the child who enters the kingdom does not stay a child. We are baptized into a *royal priesthood*, and the final image in the Scriptures is a wedding, where God's children have grown up and become kings and priests, brides of the Lamb, and the New Jerusalem comes down from heaven like a bride for her husband, and all tears are wiped away, and everyone lives happily ever after. And unless we unblushingly offer this image to our children and embrace it for ourselves, the Good News we preach is no news at all, and certainly not good.

We cannot afford to keep fooling around in Sunday school, preaching a "kiddie gospel" to our children—a gospel that hides the bitter realities and glorious promises of Scripture behind ranks of clean and happy children singing "Jesus Loves Me." We must not give them a God who turns out to be just another grown-up—who says "There, there" without really listening to their fears of the monsters under the bed, who cares only about whether or not they are being "good." We must not keep exhorting our children to be good and kind and patient and grateful and glad and loving, without offering them the faith and hope to fuel that love.

PART ONE

# Tell Me a Story

*Images of Faith and Hope*

Chapter 1

# The Death That Heals

ONCE UPON A TIME, there lived a king and queen who had three sons. One day, the king was out hunting, and he caught a huge she-eagle, and brought her home for his sons to play with. The older sons were mean and cruel, and they tormented the eagle, until one day the youngest son, Bernadet, could stand it no longer and set her free. She rewarded him by giving him a whistle made from one of her feathers. Some time later, the king went out to battle and was wounded. He lay in his bed in the palace, beyond the help of all the physicians in the kingdom. One day, however, a mysterious stranger appeared, and going to the king's bedside, he instructed the king to send his three sons to the ends of the earth in search of the Flower of Life. Whichever of them found it would be able to heal the king, and would receive his kingdom and his riches after him.

The sons set out in three different directions to search for a year and a day. When the year was almost gone and Bernadet had searched everywhere without success, he remembered the eagle's whistle and blew it. With her help, he found the Flower of Life, deep within a mountain on an island in the sea. But the flower was growing at the end of a long, narrow passage, and he could not grasp it. Despairing, he returned to the eagle, and she told him that he must cut off her right leg and use it to grasp the Flower of

Life. At first Bernadet refused, but the eagle would not be dissuaded, so Bernadet took his knife and cut off her leg, and with it he plucked the Flower of Life. With one of the flower's three blossoms, he healed the eagle's leg; the second, at her insistence, he put in his pocket. Then, holding the third blossom, Bernadet ran to meet his brothers and go home to his father.

The first one to meet him was the eldest brother. When he heard that Bernadet had been successful and would now inherit the kingdom, the eldest brother was so enraged that he seized the flower from him, and taking his knife, he fell upon his brother and killed him, and buried his body in the sand by the seashore. Then he took the Flower of Life and returned to meet the middle brother. Together they went home, where the eldest brother healed their father and received great honor and acclaim.

But one hair of Bernadet's head remained unburied. When the sun struck it, it sprang from the ground and grew into a forest of musical reeds. A shepherd passing by plucked one reed and made a flute, and when he blew it, it sang:

> O Shepherd, O Shepherd, your breath gives me life;
> To cure my father I journeyed, and found the Flower of Life.
> O Shepherd, O Shepherd, beneath the sand I lay;
> The eldest brother with his knife the youngest brother did slay.

The shepherd wandered about the kingdom, playing the flute. One day he happened to play beneath the palace window, and the king heard its song. He called the shepherd into the palace and questioned him; the shepherd handed the flute to the king to try it for himself. Played by the king, then the queen, then the middle brother, the flute made the same accusation. The king in great haste sent for his eldest son, and forced him to play the flute, which sang:

> My Brother, my Brother, you took away my life;
> To cure our father I journeyed, and found the Flower of Life.
> My Brother, my Brother, beneath the sand I lay;
> It was you who with your knife poor Bernadet did slay.

When he heard this, the king commanded that his eldest son be put into the dungeon. Then he hurried to the seashore, dug in the sand, and uncovered the body of his son. The boy was cold and still, and the father wept bitterly. But when the father's tears fell onto the boy's eyes, they opened, and he was restored to life. In great joy, father and son returned home, and in time Bernadet inherited the kingdom and ruled wisely and well.

But even if Bernadet had lain under the sand for a thousand years, he would still have been alive. For do you remember what he had in his pocket? The Flower of Life.

Every year on the day before Palm Sunday our church school holds an all-day session we call Palm Saturday. The whole day is set aside to explore the mystery of Holy Week and Easter through worship, crafts, drama, singing, and storytelling. A regular part of the schedule is the showing of a movie or video right after lunch. Several years ago, in place of the film, we played a wonderful recording of this Majorcan fairy tale, *The Flower of Life*.[1] When we began the record, the room was full of the rustling of paper wrappers, the crunching of potato chips, whispered conversations, and the general fidgeting of some two dozen children from four to fourteen years old. But as the storyteller began to say, "...And to make sure that Bernadet would never tell, the oldest brother drew his knife, and he killed Bernadet," the room was suddenly perfectly still, and the stillness did not relax until the moment when Bernadet was restored to his father. The story had woven its spell. Suddenly, the children knew, like Moses, that they were on holy ground.

What is it that is holy about this story—that fills us with awe and wonder, with a sense of being cleansed and purified, of drawing near to something tremendously significant, beautiful, and life-giving?

The obvious answer—and the reason that we chose the story for Palm Saturday—is that both Bernadet and the eagle are a little bit like Jesus. The eagle risks her life to help Bernadet; Bernadet gives his life to heal his father, and his sacrifice has the power to heal not only his father but also himself and the whole kingdom. Bernadet and the eagle are both "Christ figures," characters of great gentleness whose undeserved or voluntary suffering has the power to heal and transform.

Yet that does not explain their power over our imagination unless we already know Christ, and know why his own story holds such power over our imagination. But do even we, who hold him as our Lord, really know this? Why does the story of Jesus, any more than the story of Bernadet, overwhelm us so? What is there in his death that we recognize as holy—that fills us with joy and peace?

The story of Jesus and the story of Bernadet draw their power from the same source. The story of Bernadet will move us deeply even if we have never heard of Jesus, because we are human, and human beings in every time and place seem to be possessed of an unshakeable conviction that the only medicine to heal the waste land in which we find ourselves is the voluntary death of the innocent. From Isaiah's vision of the Suffering Servant to the "honored dead" of the Gettysburg Address, we read the record of this conviction: that if we could just find the One Good Death, the self-offering entirely without compulsion, without arrogance, and without masochism, we would unleash a power for good that would heal and restore the whole world.

We have only to say "He laid down his life" or "They died so that we might live," to experience some of the incredible potency of this unarticulated knowledge in each of us. Political propaganda has exploited it, shallow sentimentality has trivialized it; but that knowledge remains deep in our hearts: the knowledge that our healing will come, if it comes at all, through the perfect self-oblation of another. This conviction is not rational, nor is it subject to analysis and explanation. Those who desire signs and seek after wisdom will pretend they don't share it: they will find fairy tales unrealistic and ancient rituals incomprehensible. They will see in the cross of Christ a scandal or a puzzle, a legalistic transaction to appease an implacable or sadistic god, or an unhappy ending to an

otherwise inspiring life, or a temporary setback on the way to a fac-
ile immortality. But to the children, until we civilize them out of it,
the healing death of Bernadet and the slaying of the Lamb are no
stumbling block. They are the Holy. If you speak of them to children without waffling, you will invariably find that they are trans-
fixed. They are enchanted. You can hear a pin drop.

On Palm Saturday the story of Bernadet led us into the story of
Jesus. We began the morning with a bulletin board "map" of Jerusalem (highly stylized, with no attempt at archaeological accuracy).
An arched gate, houses for Pilate and the High Priest, a house with
an upper room, a hill outside the city wall and a garden for the
tomb had been cut from construction paper during Lent by one
Sunday School class, and stapled to the background. The same
class also cut out figures—Jesus, the donkey, the disciples, the table
in the upper room, Pilate, soldiers, the three crosses, the angel, the
holy women. Backed with folded masking tape, the figures could
be placed and replaced on the backdrop fairly easily. Limited, but
very effective, sound effects were provided by taped excerpts from
our Lenten program's dramatic readings of Dorothy Sayers' radio
dramas, *The Man Born to be King*.

I told the story, moving the figures around and stopping now
and then for the tape to provide the noise of the crowd shouting,
"Crucify! Crucify!" and the blows of the hammer falling. At the
end, I played the finale from *Godspell*: "Long live God...long live
God...long live God...long live God...." The children watched
spellbound, as I moved aside the cardboard stone and out came
the little white-robed cardboard Jesus. Then we split up into
groups and made banners, baked bread and cookies, decorated
Easter eggs, and prepared a little play of the entry into Jerusalem, a
short liturgical dance, and a diorama of the empty tomb. In the afternoon we came together to celebrate the eucharist and show each
other what we had done.

Palm Sunday went by, and Holy Week, and Easter Day. The
time came for Sunday school to meet again. As I thought about

what to do in the first class since Palm Saturday, I realized that we had told the story over and over, but I had made no effort to explore with the children what it all meant. I was quite embarrassed by this oversight: after all, I'm supposed to be a teacher—I should have "taught" them something. So I came prepared to sit down with my class of fourth and fifth graders and consider: what difference does it make to us, today, that this man died in this way at that time in that place? Why do we care? How does it change things between us and God?

I got nowhere. They just sat there. They had no ideas; they were tongue-tied, even hostile. The same children who were so enchanted by the story when it was given to them *as* a story, were complete blanks when I tried to get them to analyze why that story meant so much.

I felt like a failure, but I learned something. My first instinct had been sound: the power of the gospel is not, primarily, that it gives us the tools for an intellectual understanding of our relationship with God. Its power is imaginative, and speaks to our inmost feelings in ways that even as adults we can hardly describe. Indeed, we shrink from such description.

It is not only very hard to explain how Christ's suffering and death bring about our salvation; it may, with children, actually do harm to try. The psychoanalyst Bruno Bettelheim, in his book on the meaning and importance of fairy tales, tells us:

> Explaining to a child why a fairy tale is so captivating to him destroys the story's enchantment, which depends to a considerable degree on the child's not quite knowing why he is delighted by it. Adult interpretations, correct as they may be, rob the child of the opportunity to feel that he, on his own, through repeated hearing and ruminating about the story, has coped successfully with a difficult situation.[2]

For Christians, the stories of Christ's life, death, and resurrection are the most powerful "fairy tale" or "myth" in the world. They also happen to be true. But it is the enormous power of these stories that exerts such a pull on our imaginations and drives us to act them out in springtime, and Sunday by Sunday throughout the year. "Christ has died, Christ is risen, Christ will come again"; "Take and eat: this is for you." This story, which is "so captivating" to adult and child alike, though we cannot put our finger on why it so moves and exalts and nourishes us, is what we share with each other in the life of the church; and the "difficult situation" it helps us "cope with" is our own mysterious, inexplicable life: our birth, our alienation, our need for love, our fear of death, and our assurance that the Christ who died and rose again has somehow brought us home to the heart of God.

We can rob this story of its power by telling it badly, by sentimentalizing or sensationalizing or distorting it, or by analyzing or reducing it to a theological formula, or a lesson to be learned to please the teacher. We cannot rob it of its power merely by telling it too often. It deserves to be told—our children deserve to experience it—over and over again, directly as gospel and liturgy, and also as it is mirrored in fairy tale, myth, and other works of art. And our children deserve the opportunity to respond to this story, with clay, paint, and crayons, with their bodies and their voices, with their imaginations and their hearts, in worship, in sacrament, in celebration, and in play.

# NOTES

1. *Laura Sims Tells Stories Just Right for Kids*, KRL 1008 LP, KRC 1008 cassette, from Kids' Records, Box 670, Station A, Toronto, Ontario M5W 1G2 Canada.

2. Bruno Bettelheim, *The Uses of Enchantment* (New York: Knopf, 1976), p. 18.

# Chapter 2

# Tell Me a Story

WHEN OUR FIRST daughter, Grace, was two and a half, one of her favorite books was *Sylvester and the Magic Pebble*, by William Steig. Sylvester Duncan is a young donkey who lives with his mother and father and is a passionate collector of pebbles. One rainy day he finds an especially attractive one, and, holding it in his hoof as the rain beats cold on his back, he idly wishes that the rain would stop. It does. The pebble is magic: whatever Sylvester wishes as he holds the pebble comes true.

In great excitement, Sylvester starts home—only to encounter a hungry lion barring his way. "I wish I were a rock!" cries Sylvester in a panic—and he becomes a rock.

His grief-stricken parents search everywhere for him, but with no success. Finally they go home and try to pick up the pieces of their lives. Sylvester, a rock on the hillside, remains trapped and helpless as summer gives way to autumn and then winter; in the cold, dark loneliness, he falls into a long sleep.

At last, spring comes. Determined to be cheerful in spite of their great loss, Sylvester's father urges his wife to go on a picnic with him. They spread their food on a large rock—the rock that was once Sylvester. "The warmth of his own mother sitting on him" wakes Sylvester from his winter sleep, but though desperate with longing, he remains mute and helpless. The magic pebble is

15

still lying in the grass near the rock. Sylvester's father spots it and picks it up; it reminds him of his dear son. He lays it on the rock.

"Oh, how I wish he were here with us on this lovely May day," said Mrs. Duncan....Mr. and Mrs. Duncan looked at each other with great sorrow.

"I wish I were myself again, I wish I were my real self again!" thought Sylvester.

And in less than an instant, he was!

There is a joyous reunion under the brilliant orange sun, as Sylvester weeps in his mother's arms and the father capers on the grass amid the spilled picnic food. On the last page, mother, father, and child are locked in a warm, blissful embrace, eyes closed, on the family couch. Mr. Duncan has put the magic pebble in an iron safe. "Some day they might want to use it, but really, for now, what more could they wish for? They all had all that they wanted."

We read this book to Grace again and again. Each time, as the recognition scene approached, she would grow tense with excitement. We would pour all the feeling we could into Sylvester's "I wish I were myself again, I wish I were my real self again!"—then we would begin the next sentence, "...and in less than an instant..."

"HE WAS!!!" she would shout, bouncing up and down, laughing, clapping her hands. And at the peaceful, wonderfully satisfying ending, we would hug each other, too.

One day as Grace was helping me make the bed, she looked up at the crucifix on the wall. "That's Jesus," she said. "He can't get down."

"Well," I answered, "he could have gotten down. But he loved us and he wanted to save us, so even though it hurt, he stayed there."

"He died."

"Yes, he did. And they put him in a tomb. And do you remember what happened next?"

She thought for a minute.

"He rose from the dead!" Then louder, triumphantly, "He became himself again! Just like Sylvester!!"

*Praeparatio evangelica,* "preparation for the gospel," was the term that the Latin church used for those elements in paganism—especially pagan literature and myth—that seemed to speak the truth, and to anticipate in some way the central pattern of the Christian faith. The pattern is that of death and rebirth; of victory and vindication through weakness, loss, and sacrificial love. There has always been a tension in the church between those who welcome the role of stories and myths in preparing for the gospel, and those who have felt, Why bother with *praeparatio evangelica* when you can just have the *evangelium* itself? Why tell any stories at all besides The Greatest Story Ever Told?

A couple of years ago, a priest wrote a brief piece in a diocesan newspaper. He had been asked, he said, to give a talk on developing children's spirituality. His short answer ("flip but true") had been, "Give them A. A. Milne, the Brothers Grimm, Kenneth Grahame, J. M. Barrie, Oscar Wilde, C. S. Lewis, J. R. R. Tolkien, Shel Silverstein, and Ursula LeGuin...and get out of their way." In a later issue of the diocesan paper, someone responded with indignation. It was irresponsible of the church, this reader claimed, to hold up imaginative literature as a way of building children's spirituality. Why settle for inadequate symbols for the truth when you can give them the Truth itself? The only appropriate way of kindling children's devotion is to offer them Jesus Christ, through the Bible and the church. Everything else is at best wasted, at worst misguided.

One sees this view at its most extreme in such inventions as *The Christian Mother Goose,* in which an entire volume of the familiar nursery rhymes has been rewritten to extol Jesus, and/or good, loving behavior, as the last word for every situation, as if there were nothing whatever in God's creation that we can allow children to think about, wonder about, laugh about, or puzzle about except the single truth, "Christ is the answer." Much more subtly, and at the opposite end of the cultural spectrum, one sees the same narrow literalism at work in another trend called "bibliotherapy," which involves writing or choosing books for children based on their avowed capacity to help children through a crisis, to impart information or values, or to improve their self-image. In both these approaches, the story itself has no real existence. It is only a vehicle for a lesson whose content is at once pedestrian and abstract: "Jesus saves." "Obey your parents." "Don't accept rides from strangers." "Girls can be just as smart/athletic/enterprising as boys." "The kid who seems unfriendly may just be lonely." "Your parents' divorce is not your fault."

The stories that fill our Sunday school curriculums nearly all fall into one or both of these categories. They are told not because of their power as stories, but to advance the lesson's agenda. Bible stories themselves are told under a similar rubric: as a vehicle for a "lesson" that can be abstracted from the story and expressed (for the teacher's approval) in twenty words or less.

The imparting of information or moral lessons to children is a worthy goal. And it is fine and laudable to use a reasonably well-told story about children in real-life situations as a way of providing reassurance, insight, or compassion to young readers who are experiencing some of the same problems or uncertainties. But the kind of learning or reassurance thus provided, while it may be valuable in specific situations, is shallow and glib. Real, lasting learning, and the claiming of a real, lasting hope, take work. And children do their work through play: through projecting themselves into imagined worlds and working out the implications of that projection. To invite such work, the imagined world must be rich, complex, and compelling, like the world of *Sylvester and the Magic Pebble*.

Watching my children, I have begun to learn to tell which stories will become part of their world—will be their own, personal *praeparatio evangelica*. They may read with pleasure realistic novels about children like themselves, and draw limited lessons and valid reassurances from them. But the stories that will stay with them, feed their imaginations, and form their worldview are the stories they begin to act out—that become the subject of "pretend" play with deep absorption for the whole of a rainy afternoon. Fairy tales, adventure stories, fantasy, C. S. Lewis's *Narnia* books, Laura Ingalls Wilder's *Little House* series, the Bible: these stories open worlds that are richer, deeper, more vivid, more stirring, than the pedestrian world of contemporary realistic novels.

The church learned long ago to build its ritual, its sacred space, and its prayer out of a tissue of scriptural images, echoes, and themes. It restricts exposition to one liturgical place—the sermon—leaving the scriptural story, for the most part, to speak directly to the senses and the imagination. The Sunday school, on the other hand, has felt compelled to explain everything and thus to rob children of the opportunity to work out the meaning of the stories for themselves. When it has the courage, instead, to concentrate on simply *telling the story*, with all the love and attention and depth and authenticity it can muster, and without reducing it to a lesson—when, in short, the Sunday school borrows the mode of the liturgy—children come home from church and set to work living the story out. We have had three generations of the children of Abraham inhabit our backyard on one Sunday afternoon. We have had the annunciation, the nativity, and the flight into Egypt vividly imagined and acted out, with costumes, props, and friends pressed into service. I think we're on the right track—after all, how did Jesus teach? Ah, yes—he told stories.

# Chapter 3

# More Than Metaphor

I T IS ONE OF OUR CULTURE'S most curious assumptions that an idea needs to be part of our personal or daily experience in order to have real power for us. Earnest writers of textbooks and children's novels, liturgies and Sunday school materials, persist in this odd notion in spite of the obvious preference of nearly all children—and many adults—for fantasy worlds that range from dragons and unicorns to space invaders, romantic novels, and major league baseball. Daily life does not provide today, and rarely has provided at any time, a range of experience that feeds our imaginations richly enough to suit us: we will always, until we are trained out of it, go searching through stories, dreams, imagination, and fantasy, for worlds that are more vivid, more colorful, more scary, more inspiring, more challenging. If children are encouraged in this pursuit, instead of being taught to fear and denigrate it, and if they have access to imaginary worlds that are rich and complex instead of sentimental, sensational, or simplistic, they will learn to transcend the compass of their own experiences and assumptions. Denied these opportunities, and the humility and openness they bring, both children and adults become locked in a terrible provincialism that keeps them from learning anything they do not already think they know.

The church is heir to a specific tradition, recorded in specific, historical texts. Of the central images we find in our Scriptures and use in our liturgy, many do not relate directly to our daily lives. Others may have misleading associations because of changes in society or the unpredictable personal experiences of individuals. Few important words or concepts in Scripture are so clear and simple and emotionally transparent that they never change their meaning from century to century or context to context. To censor liturgical language on the grounds that its images no longer relate to our daily lives, is to leave ourselves only two choices: we must either replace those images with new ones, or replace them with abstract terms that purport to convey the essential meaning of the original image. Both of these expedients are frequently justified by referring to scriptural language as "metaphorical."

"Metaphor," in this sense, is taken to mean "a concrete image used to convey an abstract idea"—with the implicit assumptions that this same idea could equally well be conveyed by some other concrete image, and that the idea itself can be isolated from any concrete image, and be completely and accurately expressed in language that uses no concrete images at all. But this is a serious misunderstanding of metaphorical language, either in the Bible or elsewhere.

*Metaphor is not simply a kind of decorative language which is there to be decoded into "concepts" or "truths" or spiritual ideas and then discarded now that we have uncovered its essential point.* Rather, *the metaphor itself carries the truth.* To say that when Jesus called God "Father" he was simply looking for a memorable way to convey the truth that God cares for us, is to turn the metaphor inside out. We are meant to *experience* the image, "Father," in all its human richness and complexity, and from this experience, to derive a deep conviction (deeper than words) that it is part of God's very being to reach out to us in love—because that is what fathers do. So do mothers, and teachers, and grandparents, and favorite aunts...but the *flavor* of each kind of love is somehow subtly different.

So are the other aspects of the image. "Father" also contains the ideas of procreation, responsibility, authority, kinship, intimacy. This entire, unique complex of its elements comprises the "meaning" of the metaphor; it is not reducible to any one kernel of abstract truth that we can extract from it. If our own experience of fathers does not support that abstract conviction, we must then try to correct its effect on us in the light of what we intellectually know it is supposed to mean. But we will never, by this means, recapture the real impact of the metaphor.

Because languages and cultures change, and people's experiences vary, such correction will, no doubt, always be necessary to some degree. That does not make it desirable. If all or most of the words we find in Scripture and use in worship need to be commented on and corrected in order to yield meaning that is not seriously distorted, then we have a shockingly crippled language in which to express our faith.

But the answer does not lie, even if it were possible, in finding alternative words and images that are at once so contemporary and so bland and emotionally unambiguous that they will never need such commentary. The answer lies instead in enriching and educating our imaginations so that the words and images can regain their lost power for us—whether or not they fully correspond to our personal experience.

The kingship of God or Christ is not a concept that relates immediately to our daily lives. We have never experienced the emotions of loyalty, excitement, and awe that accompany fervent allegiance to a real sovereign. But how many people who said or sang, "The Lord is King!" either in Israel or later in Christian Europe, had actual personal experience of the royal court? Surely for them too the concept of "king" was made up primarily of elements from their imaginations—elements that also found expression in the legions of folk tales and fairy tales involving kings and queens, princes and princesses, that people told to nourish the imaginations of themselves and their children. The ability of the idea of "king" to stir the human imagination is what gave the real king much of his power—not the other way around.

Most important of all, where real experience of real political kings has entered into people's conception of the kingship of God, it is not helpful but harmful. The prophets knew from bitter experience that real kings are no better or holier than the rest of us—that in fact power corrupts and absolute power corrupts absolutely. The king they waited for so eagerly was a different kind of king—one who would take away the dominion of the bestial kings of this earth, one before whom, as Isaiah says, kings would shut their mouths. The entire New Testament can be read as a record of Jesus' struggle to redeem the image of "king" from the distortions imposed on it by political realities and reveal to the world its true meaning. And on every side he was frustrated by his hearers' lack of understanding.

Jesus tells Pilate, "My kingship is not of this world; if it were, my servants would fight." Jesus' own disciples repeatedly misunderstand and misuse the image of his kingship; seated at his table at the Last Supper, they start arguing about which of them will have the best job in the new administration that the Messiah King is going to inaugurate. And Jesus tells them, "The kings of the Gentiles exercise lordship over them, and those with the most power are seen as the most admirable. But if you belong to me, it must be different with you." And he takes up a towel, and goes from one to the next, washing their feet.

Jesus did not respond to his hearers' incomprehension by dropping the image of "king" for something simpler, more abstract, less likely to confuse. Instead, he kept telling stories, to flesh out its meaning through his hearers' imaginations; and finally, he acted the story out himself, with a bowl of water and a towel, with bread and wine, with a crown of thorns and a cross.

Stop for a moment and become as little children—as Jesus told us to do—and remember your fairy tales. Fairy tales are not an escape world of "make-believe." Told by generations of parents to their children, they are the key to our deepest emotional lives.

In fairy tales, what distinguishes a king is not that he is rich or lives in a palace or has servants to do his bidding. Certainly it is not that he busies himself with the work of administering government, collecting taxes, monitoring palace intrigues, and putting down rebellions. The king is king because he has the power to choose. Nobody has power over him: he is above the constraints of ordinary life, autonomous and free. Even more significantly, *the king has power to grant that autonomy and freedom to others.* Kings in fairy tales (unlike real kings) are always giving away half their kingdoms, or giving their daughters in marriage, or deciding who will succeed them when they die. In other words, in the human imagination, what is important about a king is not that he exacts obedience of us, but that he can give us a gift. With his autonomy, maturity, wisdom, and strength, he can—he will—make those who please him into kings and queens, too. Those who are bold to approach and persist in faith will reach their journey's end, overcome their enemies, pass the test, achieve maturity and happiness... get married, and inherit the kingdom.

The Scriptures speak to us, adults and children alike, in this universal language of human imagination and human yearning. John's thunderous visions in Revelation break open the gospel language of kingship to offer us an image of Christ who is king because he was dead and is living—whose very being is full and complete after the most severe testing that the powers of evil could subject it to—and who now *loves us and has freed us from our sins by his blood and made us a kingdom, priests to his God and Father.* The kingship he has won for himself through his own suffering—a kingship not from this world but from the gracious world of God's eternal justice and truth—that kingship he then turns and offers to us. He offers it to us not so we can lord it over others but so that we, like him, can rejoice in God's purposes perfected in us.

The Bible calls all of us to become as children and rejoice in the ending to the greatest, and the truest, fairy tale of them all. It is the story of each one of us, raised from obscurity and poverty and shame by the King of Kings and Lord of Lords, the mystical Lamb Who Was Slain—the story of how, through his love, we will grow to maturity and be given in marriage, inherit the crown of life, and live happily ever after.

Chapter 4

# In the Beginning

**W**HEN OUR DAUGHTER Grace was three and a half, we brought her baby sister home from the hospital. Somewhere I had read that the first few weeks after the birth of a second child are among the most stressful in a family's whole life cycle, and it certainly seemed that way to us. Grace expressed her jealousy of the new baby by a hunger strike lasting almost a week, and by permanently giving up her afternoon nap, just when I was desperate for peace and quiet.

She wasn't openly hostile or destructive; most of the time, in fact, she was (consciously, at least) really trying to be helpful and nice. It was just that she was *there* all the time, when I needed her to give me a break. It seemed I was spending all my time picking up her toys and being available, or else feeling guilty and frazzled because I wasn't up to picking up toys and being available. Either way, I was exhausted and very crabby.

Grace decided to do something to cheer me up. She took every one of her small toys, wrapped them in gift wrap, and tied them round with ribbon. Then she brought them by armfuls into the bedroom where I was trying to nap, and dumped them on my bed.

The Perfect Mother, of course, would have opened each one, exclaimed over them all, and said again and again how sweet and nice it was of Mommy's big girl to give her so many lovely presents. I don't remember exactly what I said and did, but I know I wasn't the Perfect Mother. I think I opened a couple of the packages (which were secured with most of a roll of Scotch tape as well as yards of tightly knotted ribbon), and then gave up and begged her to get all this stuff off my bed, and then for heaven's sake just go away and leave me alone with the baby.

Years later, in a Bible study class on Genesis, my husband and I realized that for Grace, at least, this little episode exactly paralleled the story of Cain and Abel.

Cain, the older brother, brought his offering to God, expecting it to be accepted. Abel, the younger brother, did the same. For reasons which are never told, Abel's offering was acceptable to God, while Cain's was not. So it must have seemed to Grace: the gifts she had so laboriously wrapped and presented—her very own toys, offered to her mother to make her happy—were rejected; she herself was (she must have felt) similarly rejected. Meanwhile, here was Mommy cherishing the baby, who must have seemed to a three-year-old to have nothing of value in comparison to her own sacrificial offering. It's to Grace's credit that (unlike Cain) she did not murderously attack her sister.

The story of Cain and Abel is a myth exploring the primal roots of violence: sibling rivalry and jealousy, and the fury we all feel, not only as children but throughout our lives, when someone else is preferred before us. (The story does not explore why the other is preferred; that is not, it seems, the important question.) Behind the fury is fear: fear that preference given to another means that we ourselves are of no value, fear that we will be displaced, cast out, and forgotten; fear that in losing our exclusive position of favor, we ourselves will simply vanish. It's a shame that this story appears nowhere in the three-year lectionary, or in our usual Sunday school curriculums, because it is a story that any child can identify with. This story places children's own experience of jealousy and rage, violence and fear, in a mythic perspective that can help them accept it, come to terms with it, and begin to believe that they (and God) can control it. It's only when we try to moralize and theologize the story, out of context—to treat it as a model for how God relates to us here and now—that it leads us into trouble.

The Cain and Abel story, along with stories of the expulsion of Adam and Eve from the garden, Noah's ark, and the tower of Babel, describes some of the restraints, quarantines, and other measures resorted to by God to protect his creatures from the consequences of their own uncontrolled impulses. These are stories appropriate to the early childhood of the human race—the time when our innocence was irretrievably lost, but before we had come under the covenant of law or love. Psychologists tell us that children in fact welcome the restraints that firm, loving parents place on their behavior—that they feel reassured by the discovery that they will not be allowed to act out their aggression or other impulses in ways that will actually hurt themselves or others. Cain is punished for his murder of his brother. That is just, and right, and reassuring to children: evil should be punished. But at the same time, God marks Cain with a protective mark, so that the revenge of others over him will be contained. For the child who, in hearing the story, identifies with Cain, that, too, is reassuring.

In my Sunday school class last year, we spent a lot of time on these early stories in Genesis. I had a socially and economically mixed group of second through fifth graders with a wide range of abilities and experiences. I wanted them to make these stories their own—to add them to their personal stock of mythic patterns and be able to draw on them as they tried to understand what it means to live in a world created by a good God but fallen into alienation and pain, and struggling to accept God's call to redemption first through law and then through faith, hope, and sacrificial love.

I had the class retell or comment on each story with the help of a cassette recorder. At home with my word processor, I transcribed their retellings or interwove their comments with a transcription of the scriptural text, and printed out the resulting narrative, a few sentences to a page. (This could be done equally well with a typewriter or even by hand, of course.) I brought the pages to Sunday school and handed them around to be illustrated by the children; a duplicate printout, held in reserve, allowed children who "messed up" to start afresh if they wished. The work went slowly because the children insisted that I begin each class session by reading aloud the entire narrative, which left little time for drawing. When, after several weeks, all the pages had been illustrated, I took them home and bound them between two cardboard covers. The resulting finished books are being catalogued into the church library as a permanent record of the children's engagement with the scriptural stories.

The creation story went very easily on to tape. The children's retelling of each day of creation consisted of long lists of God's creatures, from giraffes and sunflowers to mice and Japanese beetles, and each day's account ended with a ritualistic chorus, "And God said, 'This is good!'" We stopped the tape machine after each day to review what occurred on the next day, then started it again and the children actually dictated their ideas to the machine; all I did was transcribe the final result. The illustrations were lively, whimsical, and fun.

The other Genesis myths are not patterned enough to be completely retold by the children in their own words. Instead, I taped our discussion after we had read the stories in the Bible, and printed out the story in its original form or in a simplified retelling, with the children's comments interspersed in italics. I was fascinated to find that the lyrical description of Eden with its four rivers (Genesis 2:8-14) inspired several nine-year-old girls to create elaborate and lovely aerial views or maps. When we talked of Adam and Eve's exile from paradise, some of the children's comments had an almost unbearable poignancy:

> They felt bad because they loved that place very much.
> They felt homesick.
> They felt real bad because when they went out of the garden
> they didn't know anyone there and they knew everything in the
> garden.

As it happened, our exploration of the Cain and Abel story came during the height of the Persian Gulf War. We used the story in part as a springboard for a general discussion of how to deal with anger and hate, compiling a formal list of alternatives to violent action: "You can go in a separate room and get your anger out on things that aren't alive and won't break. . . . You can try to think of good things about the person you're mad at. . . . You can try to talk to the person. . . . You can ask another person to judge between you. . . . You can pray." The finished narrative included this list, but mostly consisted of the children's spontaneous comments on the story in light of what they were hearing day by day on radio and TV:

> Cain didn't do any of these things.
> He just said, "I hate that guy! I hate that guy!"
> and he killed him.
>
> Maybe he hit him on the head.
> Maybe he used the knife that he had for cutting his crops.
> Maybe he used a cross. . . .
> There are lots and lots of ways of hurting people.
> Ever since Cain and Abel
>   people have been looking for new ways of hurting people.
> Every time we have a war
>   we find out that people have invented more new ways
>   of hurting other people.

The children's final comments blamed the Devil for tempting people to resort to violence. (In an earlier discussion they had resisted completely the idea that Saddam Hussein was so satanic it was okay to hate and kill in response to his aggression.) They acknowledged how hard it is to continue to live in relationship with someone you perceive as a rival or enemy ("Sometimes it seems easier to just get rid of the person who's bothering you"), but ended by depicting the burden of Cain's guilty conscience. When they illustrated the text, one boy added the words, "Let There Be Peace on Earth" to the title page, above the printed title which was simply "Cain and Abel: How War and Death Came into the World."

Confronting the Cain and Abel myth allowed these children to see their own angers and jealousies side by side with the world's political fury and aggression. One boy, whose relationship with his little brother was particularly rocky, worked over the story again and again with his parents during the week, with obvious fascination and relief at the discovery that he was not the first to harbor murderous fantasies toward a younger brother. With little prompting and no moral coercion, the children were able to articulate ethical principles that they presented as equally valid for themselves at home and school and for nations on the global stage. They were able to grasp the hope that their own vision of God's goodness would keep them from imitating Cain, though they acknowledged how hard such restraint can be. I could not, of course, reassure them that the adult world would learn comparable restraint any time soon.

But perhaps for just that reason, the vision that they took with them may be more real and more lasting than if it had come from a moral dictate imposed by the teacher or contained in a didactic lesson. It is their own vision, their own hope, claimed by them out of a story that they explored and tested and found to ring true. People rise up against each other; real harm is done; but God is not mocked. The story's undiluted honesty about the first two facts of life makes its affirmation of the last one more believable. Such is the power of myth; and perhaps the most lasting gift we can give our children in Sunday school is to set them free to explore these stories with implicit trust in their own response.

# Chapter 5

# Too Hard for the Lord

OVER MY DESK HANGS a small plaque, elegantly framed in gold-toned wood. It contains a simple message, in graceful, illuminated calligraphy: "Is anything too hard for the LORD?—Genesis 18:14." The plaque was given to me six years ago, a Christmas present from the rector to the Christian education staff member. I thanked him and hung it up. And in the last eighteen months I have repeatedly fought the urge to take it down.

The verse on the plaque is taken from the words of the three angels to Abraham and Sarah, after Sarah has laughed at their news that she and her husband will have a son. The angels rebuke Sarah for doubting, even after so many years of fruitless waiting. "Is anything too hard for the Lord?"

Today, as I write, is the day when our baby was supposed to be born. But we lost this baby six months ago, and that was the third such loss in one year. The second one happened just a year ago—within days of what was to have been the due date for an earlier baby, also lost. So the calendar this week bristles with loaded dates: two birthdays that never came, one anniversary of a long, painful, untimely labor that brought only emptiness.

We had had two children easily enough; we thought we could have a third anytime. Back in 1986, with a seven-year-old and a four-year-old, we decided the time was right. But for two years nothing happened at all. We were puzzled, but busy and happy enough with our family not to be particularly concerned. When I did conceive, it was rather a surprise. We told our daughters right away, partly to help us get used to the idea that after so many years we would be having a baby again.

And every night we prayed. We prayed for the new baby growing inside Mommy, we prayed for its health and its safe birth and for the grace to love it and cherish it when it would be born. The children, with typical directness, prayed explicitly that it would not miscarry. Two of their aunts had had miscarriages, and though we did not think this had any bearing on us, we could not help being aware of it.

Then the morning came when we had to tell the children that the baby was gone. Almost the first words that came from our younger daughter, through her tears, were, "All those prayers! All those prayers that the baby wouldn't be a miscarriage!"

"Is anything too hard for the Lord?"

Through Scripture, liturgy, and sacrament, the church bears witness to the mingled darkness and light of this world that God has made and Christ has made new through the blood of the cross. Week by week, we are invited to experience our own story: the story of a lovely and precious creation marred by alienation, futility, and pain; the story of God's long and costly work of calling his people and restoring them through his Son. The liturgy calls on us to cry out to the Lord for deliverance and mercy; to acknowledge our weakness and fears; to offer our gifts and our lives, to come forward to be loved and fed and sent out to live in faith. For those with ears to hear, the liturgy tells the truth: it does not bathe us in sentimental pieties or bind heavy burdens on our shoulders without giving us the strength to bear them.

But for children, the Christian community often tells a different story. At church, the children are likely to be away from the holy space, and the story comes to them as an object lesson, a moral exemplum, or a heartwarming anecdote. If they come to the altar at the eucharist, many of them receive not the transforming Body and Blood of the crucified and risen Lord, but a blessing—a kind and gentle touch, but one with much less depth and power than the Bread of Life, the Cup of Salvation.

At home, the family may pray and read the Bible, but the parents get precious little help in fostering a faith in their children that is true to the gospel, or to real life. Even our own faith is likely to be formed as much by cultural pieties as by the real content of Scripture and liturgy. For children, the virtually unanimous witness of religious publishing and our own cultural conditioning is to proclaim an easy Good News, especially for kids: a simple blessing, instead of a sacrament of life out of death. God's in his heaven, all's right with the world, is the message—and the only thing missing is that we all have to try harder to be loving. "Is anything too hard for the Lord?" Of course not! And we cross our fingers and hope that nothing will force us to question whether it's really so—instead of accepting that our children are called to travel with us through the hard and bitter mystery of the creation as it actually is.

After my first miscarriage, several kind friends reproached us for telling our children about the pregnancy so soon. "If you hadn't told them you were pregnant, you wouldn't have had to tell them about the miscarriage at all," they argued. "Think of all the pain you could have spared them." By the third pregnancy, these voices had become so loud that we heeded them, at least in part. We decided to say nothing until we were safely past the point where the other two had failed...if indeed we reached that point.

But our older daughter guessed what was going on. She didn't tell us she had guessed; she figured that if we had wanted her to know, we would have told her in the first place, so she had better not let on that she knew. Then I began to suspect that she had guessed, but I just didn't have the energy to puzzle out how to break the cycle of secrecy we had begun. By the time we knew, once again, that there was no hope, we were all exhausted by weeks of whispering and guessing. The idea of continuing that game, and making up some other explanation for why I had to go to the doctor and then spend the next day in bed, was just absurd. But there were those who urged us to do just that, to spare the kids.

We cannot shelter our children from the pain in our common life. There is much too much of it, and children are not fools. When something is wrong, they know it, and they would rather know why Mommy is crying, and offer to share her burden in love, than worry about it all by themselves and imagine all kinds of scary possibilities. Perhaps if Mommy were a better actress she would simply not cry, or at least not in front of the kids. But I don't believe that God calls individuals or families to that kind of bravado.

Yet the kind of honesty that God does call us to is not simple or easy. Again and again in the last year and a half, that plaque over my desk has challenged me: "Is anything too hard for the Lord?" It's a question that begs a question. Are you lacking in faith? Are you presuming to criticize? Is God saying, "Well, if that's all you think of me, no wonder I can't help you"? If I had really believed God's promises, prayed with more perfect faith, would I have somehow forestalled those losses? If I really felt, now, "thy will be done," would I be filled with grateful serenity instead of with anger, confusion, and grief?

It's not easy to fight our cultural and spiritual conditioning, unmask the false gospels, and claim the story that is actually told in the Scriptures and the creeds. The angels asked Abraham and Sarah, "Is anything too hard for the Lord?" and we can, if we choose, just leave that question dangling, with all its potential to blame the victim when God seems absent, helpless, inscrutable, or even cruel. Or we can search the Scriptures for their own perspectives on faith and hope, that challenge the simplistic pieties so often peddled to adults and children alike:

> By faith Abraham obeyed when he was called to go out to a place which he was to receive as an inheritance, and he went out, not knowing where he was to go. By faith he sojourned in the land of promise, as in a foreign land, living in tents with Isaac and Jacob, heirs with him of the same promise. For he

looked forward to the city which has foundations, whose builder and maker is God....

For these all died in faith, not having received what was promised, but having seen it and greeted it from afar, and having acknowledged that they were strangers and exiles on the earth. For...they desire a better country, that is, a heavenly one. Therefore God is not ashamed to be called their God, for he has prepared for them a city.
(Heb. 11:8-10, 13, 16)

For many centuries, most Christians saw in this passage the very essence of their faith. It was this belief that gave meaning to their lives and that they passed on, with great conviction, to their children. Today we have almost ceased to speak this language. It still surfaces in hymns and liturgy, and flourishes in isolated contexts like sympathy cards. But it rarely contributes to our day-to-day self-understanding as people of faith who are trying to live in hope and love. It is thoroughly out of fashion in most pulpits and in nearly all Sunday school materials, and many parents shy from emphasizing it with their children. We have become so wary of "pie in the sky when you die" that we have taught ourselves to look only to the here and now for evidence of the goodness, love, and purposes of God. Our faith and hope are to be grounded in looking around at nature, family, friendships, our own healthy bodies and unique personalities, and concluding from what we see that God is faithful and good.

While things are going well for us, this doesn't work too badly. After all, we do not feel much like strangers and exiles on the earth; we are not exactly pining for our heavenly country. We have plenty to thank God for, and we are pretty conscientious about remembering to be grateful, and trying to do the kingdom's work. We can see in our own happiness and fulfillment much evidence of God's gracious plan. We ground our *faith* in the confidence we gain from that happiness, and our *hope* in the expectation that it will continue; and out of this spiritual affluence we draw the energy to *love* God and our neighbor (especially our less fortunate neighbor) as we feel we ought.

If we just don't think too much about other people's troubles, they will not seriously challenge our confidence in God's unfailing kindness to us, his children. If we remind our children again and again how lucky they are and how thankful they should feel that God takes such good care of them—and if we are careful to shield them from as much pain as we possibly can, even if it means telling them lies—then we can go on for years like this. That is why it is such a shock when we first find a major roadblock across our path, disrupting our happy, rewarding pilgrimage, our "normal life."

Our ancestors in faith called this life a "vale of tears." Though we may dislike that expression as being a bit extreme, at least for favored folks like us, we must admit with John Bunyan in *Pilgrim's Progress* that there are few of us for whom the landscape has not at some time included the Slough of Despond, the Hill Difficulty, Doubting Castle, and, often enough, the Valley of the Shadow of Death. Our way through this world is not always straightforward, manageable, or fun. God does not promise that it will be. It is our own culture, and frequently our own church, full of false promises and pious reassurances, that has deceived us, so that our faith depends on our satisfaction with our life right now.

In our family and in the lives of all God's children everywhere, there are many things that seem to have proved too hard for the Lord. The world is full of disaster and waste. Prayers offered in faith go ungranted; children suffer dreadfully. God tantalizes us with promises we scarcely looked for, and then yanks them away. My casual expectation that our lives would go on being intelligible and fulfilling—and my confident imparting of that same expectation to my children—is gone. If that is what faith means, if that's what I have to believe in order to live with the question, "Is anything too hard for the Lord?" then I flunk the test. And the gospel in which I had put my trust flunks the test, too. The plaque can go in the garbage can.

But understood in another way, I can leave that verse up on the wall. The story in Genesis does not tell us what answer Sarah gave to the angels' challenge, as, old and dried up, she found herself expected to believe without a struggle that God would give her the son he had denied her so long. Perhaps she said, "Yes," or "Maybe," and out of compassion for her long sojourn in the desert of broken hopes they forbore to argue with her. Whatever her reply, those who later looked to Abraham and Sarah as their ancestors in faith chose to remind us that their faith was confirmed though they died without seeing its fulfillment. And so will we. At the heart of faith is the conviction that God is the builder and maker of the city, and that nothing, finally, is too hard for the Lord—not the conviction that it will all work out for us while we are still strangers and exiles on the earth.

I can leave that verse up on the wall because "hard" can also mean "hard saying," or "hard place," and in that sense, truly nothing is too hard for the Lord. There is no place that is too terrible, too sad, too difficult, for the Lord to be there with us—the Lord who wept with Mary and Martha and sweated blood in Gethsemane. For us, at least, it has proved essential that however hard the place, we are there together before our God, adults and children, telling the truth, and not trying bravely to protect each other or vaunt a pious assurance we do not really hold. God has his own ways of easing the hard places for us and our children. Telling lies is no help to anybody.

# PART TWO

# The Distorted Canon

## *Unmasking the Kiddie Gospel*

# Chapter 6

# The Distorted Canon

W E ALL WANT OUR children to know and love the Bible—to claim as their own the story of God calling his people into covenant and redemption through the history of Israel and the life and death of Jesus. We would like to give them the Scriptures in a form that is accessible to their age group, attractively illustrated, accurate, and so inviting that they will spend hours poring over it, gradually forging connections between the stories of the Old and New Testaments, the life of the church, the events of their own lives, and their own inner life of wonder, questioning, delight, hope, fear, love, prayer, and moral choice. This, after all, is what the Scriptures do for the people of God. But one doesn't necessarily just walk into a bookstore and take such a volume off the shelf.

There is a subtle but genuine disjunction for most American Episcopalians between their idea of "the Bible" and their experience of the Christian life through prayer, liturgy, and the community of faith. Bible publishing in the United States and popular-culture images of the Bible are heavily influenced by the large and pervasive tradition of American evangelical theology, with its literal interpretive style, its emphasis on rote learning of Bible texts, Bible mottoes, Bible lore, and Bible trivia, and its isolation of Scripture from the context of church history, liturgy, and tradition. The very words, "the Bible," to Americans, carry a freight of imagery from the evangelical subculture—a sense of entering a world of muscular characters in robes and sandals, of bright colors and action-packed poses, of epic encounters and supernatural events. This is all the more true for children, since selection, retelling, illustration, and design so thoroughly determine the form under which the Word reaches children.

It is possible, of course, to give a child a Bible that is just that—the complete Old and New Testaments, unabridged, in a readable translation, or paraphrased to simplify the language while altering the content as little as possible. This is a *sine qua non* for older children who read fluently and with enjoyment, especially if they also own one or more children's Bibles, or selections of Bible stories that indulge in extensive retelling, imaginative elaboration, or moral commentary. Good readers of ten or eleven are ready to explore the Scriptures in solitude: dipping, skimming, or reading in depth as the Spirit moves. Here the most important element is the text itself. Pictures and even introductory material should take a subordinate place, and the child should be left free to meet the text on its own terms. The translation should reveal some of the style of the ancient originals, especially the Hebrew text—its elusiveness, its vivid metaphors, its poetic use of parallelism, its elaborate courtly paraphrases, its fierce cursing and rich blessing, its heights and depths.

For younger children, for reading aloud, or for reading cover to cover, there is a place for the children's Bible, or collection of Bible stories. But it is here that American publishers, even those from catholic traditions, seem to be captive to a seriously reductive view of the Scriptures and of children's spirituality. You will look long and hard before you find a children's Bible that represents the full spectrum of the canon—especially as the canon informs the liturgy and the church's year.

The standard children's Bible is all narrative. It moves slowly and with considerable detail (and often extratextual commentary) through Genesis—creation and fall, Cain and Abel, Noah, the tower of Babel, and the Abraham, Isaac, Jacob, and Joseph stories—and Exodus, dwelling with loving detail on the plagues of

Egypt and the crossing of the Red Sea. But then the narrative begins to get skimpy.

Following a rehearsal of the Ten Commandments (rarely is any of the rest of the Law represented), the story flits through Joshua and Judges, then skips to a more or less detailed account of the stories of Samuel, Saul, and David, a brief mention of Solomon and the Temple, some quick references to the later monarchies and their decadence, perhaps a couple of the Elijah stories, one or two psalms (often incorporated into the David story), and a few paragraphs from the prophets. After a mention of the destruction of Jerusalem, the Old Testament typically comes to rest with the Daniel stories, or possibly with Jonah or Esther. Then, with a new title page—and often a change in illustrator and style—we jump into the more familiar New Testament world.

The gospels (chiefly the synoptics) are merged into a single narrative, which may or may not include a sampling of Jesus' parables and sayings, as well as his miracles. The events of Holy Week are told at length, but the resurrection appearances are usually limited to the first moments at the empty tomb. Many editions draw to a close somewhere between Easter and the conversion of Paul; others go on to narrate Paul's journeys and struggles in some detail, usually concluding with a glance at the Book of Revelation. If any selections from the epistles are included, they tend to be brief passages dealing with practical matters—ethics, church order, Christian living—interspersed among the adventures of Paul and his colleagues. The great hymns of Philippians and Colossians, the glory of the cross, the images of baptism, adoption, the Body of Christ, the great High Priest, the communion of saints, are utterly absent.

The New Testament canon in fact offers many images of Jesus, but it is as teacher and healer almost exclusively that he figures in Bibles for children. This bias—one is tempted to call it censorship—may arise from a notion that such a Christology is the only one suitable for children, or it may simply reflect the mainstream of Protestant spirituality for adults. Either way, its result will be a distortion of children's devotional lives, not only by downplaying struggle and ambiguity, but also by devaluing liturgical spirituality and communal faith and hope in favor of a narrow focus on receiving direct help for personal problems.

But the greatest problem with these children's Bibles is their distortion of the Old Testament canon, and the implications of this for children's ability to understand the Bible not as "a story," but as "my story." For the heart of the Scriptures is a continuing pattern of exile and return, of loss, hope, and restoration, of new life out of renunciation and death. And it emerges not only from narrative, but from prophecy, psalm, and hymns; from vision and exhortation; from parable, image, and metaphor.

This pattern recurs in the Hebrew Bible in three great movements. The first is the primeval exile from the Garden of Eden, echoed and extended into hope in the call to Abraham to leave his kindred and his country and seek a land of promise. The second is the bondage in Egypt of the children of Israel, their deliverance in the Exodus, their entry into the land, and the building of Jerusalem, the joy of the whole earth. The third is the faithlessness of the people, the destruction of Jerusalem, the Babylonian Captivity, and the promise, beyond hope, that the dry bones will live, the people return to their land, the walls of Jerusalem be rebuilt, the union of God and his people be celebrated as a marriage feast of everlasting joy.

It is the last of these movements that has, historically, most enriched the vocabulary of the church. The prophecies of Second Isaiah and Ezekiel, the poetry of Lamentations and the psalms, the love affair of the people of God with Jerusalem, their anguish at her destruction, and their hope of her renewal forge the link between the Hebrew Scriptures and the New Testament, make intelligible the figure of the Messiah, inform Jesus' parables and sayings, and gloss the visions of Revelation. The church turns to these scriptural images in prayer and supplication, in awaiting the Savior and celebrating his coming, and in the paschal season at Tenebrae and the Great Vigil of Easter. It is these strands of Scripture that lie behind much of Jesus' own spirituality. It is these strands of scriptural imagery that have the power to reach beyond the external details of exciting adventures and archaeological scenery to stir children's hearts deep down, in the same places as are stirred by folk tales and fairy tales and the best imaginative literature.

Children know that our life on earth is itself the story of exile and loss; they have all known the loss of their own paradisal babyhood and the coming of frustration, guilt, alienation, and pain. They know that their greatest need is to find their way home to where they will be welcomed, loved, and fed, and to come of age, inherit the kingdom, receive the crown of life, and know that all tears are forever dried and all that was lost has been found. When children are exposed to lectionary and liturgy throughout the church year, the images that most captivate them include the Garden of Eden, the Flood, the Exodus and Sinai; the City of God, the holy mountain where swords are beaten into ploughshares and all tears are dried; the dry bones; the Good Shepherd; the cross and empty tomb; the wedding feast and the New Jerusalem.

One of my daughters, at two and a half, became obsessed with the story of the raising of Lazarus, and insisted that I draw her a "crying Jesus" to take to bed with her every night for a week. The other, at almost four, showed the same kind of fascination with the vision of the dry bones from Ezekiel, which she had seen acted out in our parish's Easter pageant. She made me read it to her over and over, until she almost knew it by heart; I once overheard her in her room, chirping to herself, "And the dry bones said, 'Son of man, can we live?' And the Son of man said, 'Of course you can!'" I have never met a child who was not enchanted by the vision of the Peaceable Kingdom, or deeply moved by the promise (so utterly immediate and understandable to children) that God would wipe away all tears from our eyes. Yet I have found no children's Bible now in print that includes all these images, and the overwhelming majority include none of them.

In Sunday school and in devotional Bible reading at home, we are likely to violate the story even further by telling it in snippets, out of order, and treating it chiefly as a source of themes and moral maxims. Suppose we told the story of *Cinderella* that way—breaking it up into a dozen discrete little episodes, scrambling their

order, failing to introduce the characters, and then telling these episodes from time to time in ways that were either heavy with moral
import or bland, cute, and sentimental? Suppose we ended each
episode either by explaining outright to our children what we feel
is the important meaning they should glean from the story frag-
ment, or asking them to extract it for us, for our judgment and approval? Suppose we cheered them in some little ditty about how
happy we feel when we read stories about lovely Cinderella?

Preschoolers might play along with us, because they are so eager
for stories that they will take them even on terms that insult their
intelligence and their sensibility. But would we be surprised if as
they grew and we still kept up this silly game, they became first baffled, then bored and contemptuous, or (the "good" pupils) un-
imaginatively compliant, proficient at finding in the story what they
knew we wanted them to find? And would we be surprised if the
story lost all its power over them—its power to impart hope, its
power to invite them to wonder and struggle with the meaning of
their life, and its power to suggest the tools for that struggle?

Taking a children's Bible from the shelf in a bookstore, we
must ask: What is included and what left out? What is added?
What atmosphere do the text and pictures project: awe and mystery, epic heroism, whimsical charm, novelistic realism, sentimental sweetness? Are the different literary forms so assimilated, the
narrative style so homogenized, as to invite misplaced literalism or
unnecessary skepticism? Reading the story in this version, how
would a child begin to answer the questions, What does it mean?
What is the point? Does the narrator draw moral and theological
conclusions for the reader, or try to dictate the quality of the
child's response to the story, or try to guarantee that the child's response will always be one of happy acceptance, gratitude, and optimism? How close does this version come to offering a truly
representative selection of the Scriptures, an accurate condensed
version of the story of salvation, or a full range of images for God
or for Christ, with which to wonder, ponder, and pray? In short,
does this Bible preach the gospel—or the kiddie gospel?

There is a crying need for a Bible for young readers that will open a door for them into the church's own story, so that, in family reading or quiet exploration, they will be free to "make the circuit of Zion, walk round about her, count the number of her towers..." so that they may come to love her and know that she is "the very center of the world and the city of the great king," and in turn may be able to "tell those who come after."

# Chapter 7

# Sacred Baby-Sitting

W E DON'T USUALLY think of three-year-olds as coming to church to pray, to know God, and to share Jesus' risen life. We think of them as coming to church simply because their parents are coming and can't leave them at home, or perhaps because we want them to get a sense of the flavor of Christian worship and a feeling that they belong in the worshiping community. When we think about teaching preschoolers about God, we see ourselves as imparting information about a subject previously unknown to the children and conceptually way beyond their capacity, but so important that we want to begin now anyway. We hope that something in our attitude toward the subject—our reverence, our love and care for the children—will rub off, and they will begin, dimly, to understand that the way we feel about God is special and we want them to feel that way too. Even when they are participating with full attention in a religious activity, we think of children as going through the motions, motions that we hope, as they grow, will grow with them into real meaning.

These assumptions are built into the way we design programs for young children in the parish. Nearly every parish has a nursery, where preschoolers spend all or most of their Sunday morning. It is a space that resembles a secular nursery school or playroom: there is a supply of toys; there may be something to climb on, rock in, or ride on; there are art supplies, puzzles, and books. In all likelihood there is also a worship corner—a picture of Jesus, perhaps, or a small altar with a cross and candles. Children play freely or do projects, while the teachers provide love and supervision. The toys, crafts, and morning routine may also be used to introduce Christian themes. Dolls and toy food can teach the concepts of family love and thankfulness; when a snack is served, it is preceded by a simple grace or blessing. Story time is the occasion for Bible stories or the teaching of kind and loving behavior. Singing and simple prayers emphasize thankfulness for daily blessings, trust in God, and growth in love at home, with friends, and in the world. If a curriculum is used, it is likely to focus on the child's daily experience of self, family, neighborhood, and play, and to elicit similar themes about God from these experiences.

It's no inaccuracy, and no insult, to call this approach to preschool religious education "sacred baby-sitting." With its core of free play, colored by Christian elements supplied by the teacher, it reflects and perpetuates our assumptions about the role and meaning of Christian faith and community, especially for children. That is, it leads children to think of the church's role in their lives as that of standing by and supplying moral directives to be thankful, glad, kind, and loving, and to think of God preeminently as a loving provider of daily blessings, and Jesus as an example of peaceful and patient behavior. Time set aside for activity understood as sacred—a curriculum lesson, a story, singing, or prayer—reinforces our culture's assumption that explicitly "religious" activity belongs in isolated moments, separate from normal spontaneous activity, and that it always involves sitting still, passively absorbing the interpretations of teachers, and operates almost exclusively on verbal and conceptual levels.

Imagine, instead, a nursery space that contains not only a miniature altar with cross and candles, but a child-size chalice and paten, a small font and Paschal candle—and whose shelves display no dolls, blocks, trucks, toy telephones or doctor sets, no Lego's or puzzles, no curriculum leaflets or workbooks. Instead, a series of baskets are filled with wooden or clay figures depicting the stories of Jesus' birth, his childhood visit to the Temple, his baptism, his temptation in the desert, several of his miracles, his blessing of the children, his entry into Jerusalem, the Last Supper, his burial and resurrection, and his encounters with Mary Magdalene and with the disciples on the road to Emmaus.

Imagine other baskets filled with laminated cards representing the seven days of creation and the Ten Commandments; a large box of sand to serve as the Sinai or Judean desert; a carved wooden Noah's ark; a model of the Ark of the Covenant and one of the Temple in Jerusalem; figures of Abraham and Sarah and of the people of Israel in the promised land and in exile in Babylon. Imagine boxes covered with gold foil representing parables of the kingdom, each containing brightly colored, flat cardboard figures and felt cut-outs to allow children to play imaginatively with the figures of the Good Shepherd and his sheep—the mustard seed and the tree it grows into, with nests for birds to sit in—the merchant with his pearl of great price. Imagine a tiny altar, dollhouse-sized, with cup and paten, and with figures of Jesus and the disciples to stand around it and to be interchanged with figures of the Good Shepherd and the sheep, or a vested priest and modern-day parishioners: men, women, children.

Imagine that children enter this space and sit in a circle. After a greeting and some singing, the teacher brings out one of the boxes or baskets and, using the clay figures or other solid, manipulable materials, tells in quiet and spare language today's selection from the story of God's people, and invites the children to wonder about the story's impact and meaning, without ever suggesting to them what it is supposed to mean or how it should make them feel. Then the children choose how they wish to respond: they may work with the materials for today's story or some other story; they may draw or paint or use clay or other art materials. When the time is almost over, they are called back together for conversation, prayer, and a blessing, and they enter the adult liturgy at the peace, joining their families for the gift of Christ's Body and Blood.

This description represents one adaptation of the pioneering work of Sofia Cavalletti, a disciple of Montessori who has spent over forty years exploring the ways children experience God. Her

"Catechesis of the Good Shepherd" and its offshoot, Jerome Berry-man's *Godly Play*, may be on their way to revolutionizing the ways we understand the spirituality of small children and mediate their experience of Christian worship and community. (Information about these books appears in the final chapter.)

Cavalletti's book, *The Religious Potential of the Child*, outlines her conviction that all young children have a tremendous potential for real spirituality—an intuitive sense of God and a deep longing to know God, whatever their religious training. This means that the work of the religious educator is not to introduce to children a subject they know nothing about, or to supply religious interpreta-tions for their daily lives. It is, rather, to provide them with the tools—images and stories—that will allow them to work with their own experience, and yearnings, to speculate and to wonder, and (in their own way) to build a conscious, articulate faith. Over many years of work with children, at her original center in Rome and in places as diverse as Japan, Mexico, West Africa, and North Amer-ica, she has found scriptural and liturgical images to serve as those tools: the good shepherd, the eucharist, the paschal mystery, the light of baptism; the pearl of great price, the mustard seed, the yeast in dough, the vine and its branches. Interestingly, several of these are also the images that appear again and again in the very earliest of Christian art, in the catacombs—the images that spoke most deeply to the infant church.

Jerome Berryman is a pastor and educator who studied with Cavalletti in Italy and has, since the early 1970s, been applying and adapting her methods in the United States. One of his major departures from Cavalletti's original methods is in his choice of scriptural canon: whereas her syllabus contains only New Testa-ment and liturgical material, his includes a carefully chosen se-quence of Old Testament stories, showing God's saving deeds in history. In recent years Berryman has been conducting his own workshops and publishing his own materials: *Young Children and Worship* (with Sonja M. Stewart) and *Godly Play*. *Young Children and Worship* contains detailed lesson plans and is the nearest thing to a curriculum for the ordinary parish unable to send people long distances for intensive training. Berryman is also beginning production and distribution of the many necessary materials (for which patterns are given in *Young Children and Worship*, though they are often difficult to interpret and use). This is a departure from the original Cavalletti principle of requiring the direct involvement of the local community in creating handmade materials, but it may bring the possibility of a Good Shepherd nursery within reach of many more parishes with limited resources.

The half-dozen three-to-five-year-olds who attend our parish's Good Shepherd nursery regularly are drawn to it in a way they never were to the traditional nursery. It is led by a dedicated group of parents who have read the books and organized the space and now rotate as "leaders" and "greeters" within the nursery program itself. The parents have many stories to tell of moments of insight and discovery, both within the nursery program and afterward as the children participate in the eucharist.

As an artist I have had the privilege of making many of the materials, and my own children, though much too old for the Good Shepherd nursery, insist on playing with the clay figures as they are made one by one. When I was making the dollhouse-sized figures of priest and people, my eight-year-old was home from school with a bad cold. She watched in fascination as the figures took shape, and the instant I allowed her to handle them, she was moving them around, having them pray and sing—even stopping to compose and write out a sermon for the priest to preach. We all know children who "play church." But the magnetic attraction these little figures had for my daughter made me stop and think.

Our toy stores are full of play materials covering every range of human activity, from home, school, and grocery store to hospital, farm, beauty parlor, fairy castle, space station, and wars of every conceivable type, but of course none of them represent Bible stories or worshiping communities. Evangelical supply houses have come out with "poseable action figures" of muscular scriptural heroes such as David, Daniel, and Samson. But nobody, it seems, has thought of supplying Christian families or even parish nurseries with materials for imaginative play about the story we tell every

Sunday in the creed and the Eucharistic Prayer. It had never struck me before that there was anything strange about this state of affairs, and that alone speaks volumes about the strength of our culture-bound assumptions.

Any parish, any family, can begin today to counteract these cultural distortions simply by making sure that our children, at home and at church, have among their toys a sturdy nativity set and a Noah's ark—the two scenes from Scripture that are readily available as toys. A model altar with priest and people is also easily assembled from dollhouse figures and furnishings; only the priest's vestments need be made from scratch. Even if the parish is unable to convert its nursery to a full-fledged Good Shepherd program, the introduction of some scriptural and liturgical playthings, casually included along with the dolls and trucks, will encourage the nursery children to (as Montessori would say) "work with" the faith story as they would with any other story or situation represented by their toys. Even this small incursion into their repertoire of play experiences would convey to children the message that faith does not belong only in lessons, worship time, and books, but is something that engages our hearts, hands, and imaginations as well.

Cavalletti and her followers have helped us see that what is true of every other kind of education is true of Christian education also: children learn by exploration and manipulation, by play and fantasy and wonder. The playthings they are given and the stories they are told will either increase the range of their exploration or limit it, and in this exploration the teacher is not so much an instructor as a midwife and a guide. The Good Shepherd nursery offers us an example of how to put these principles to work, building for our parish's children a wonderfully fertile environment in which the seeds of Christian faith may grow.

# Chapter 8

# Come, Risen Lord

A NYONE  WHO  HAS  browsed through the greeting card section of a neighborhood store at Eastertime can observe that our culture has difficulty expressing joy, especially for children. We tend to forget the differences between *joy, happiness,* and *fun,* and we homogenize all good wishes for all possible occasions into "Have a happy day." Even in the church, as we plan worship for children our main agenda is often that they should find it "fun." Our efforts to express the joy of the gospel in Sunday school easily become exercises in convincing children how much *fun* it is to be a Christian, and how *happy* we all feel because Jesus is our friend. At Easter, our interpretation of the joy of the resurrection is apt to suggest either a cozy, domesticated type of happiness ("Jesus' friends were so glad that he had come back to them"), or else a sort of slapstick, carnival hilarity, with great big smiles and circus-bright colors:

> Suddenly Mary was at my side,
> Pinching my ear and pulling my hair,
> And grinning as wide as a whole piece of pie.
> "Matthias!" she said, "Matthias, don't hide.
> I saw Jesus around and about and alive!...
> He's alive; He's the one who said 'Mary' to me!
> Matthias, get up and come running to see."
>
> Then Mary left, dancing and singing with glee.[1]

It is hard to find words to convey to children the elements of awe, strangeness, and fear that appear in every scriptural account of the resurrection. Words for awe and wonder are not part of the vocabulary of our kiddie subculture, and we seem reluctant to credit children with the ability to appreciate that an experience may be both *solemn* and *joyful*, or joyful without necessarily being "fun." (It's instructive to trace the history of the word *solemn*. In Latin *sollemnis* meant simply "sacred"; by medieval English the word had come to mean "festive, celebratory, splendid"; after the Reformation, it took on its modern sense of "weightily serious, grave to the point of gloom.")

On the surface, it's easiest and most plausible to explain our Easter joy to children by attributing it to the fact that *the disciples now had Jesus back with them:* now they could be *happy* again. This suggests that the resurrection served essentially to undo the crucifixion: to bring back for Jesus' friends the happy, familiar conditions they had known before that terrible blow fell across their lives. It seems like a simple, reassuring, comforting way to explain the meaning of Easter to children, for it hints that the crucifixion was like a bad dream that fades away with the light of dawn—a terrible, scary thing that threatened to destroy our happiness but then turns out not to have really mattered after all.

This version of the story not only underestimates children's capacity to understand and appreciate *solemn joy*—awe, wonder, fear and trembling, mystery, unanswered questions that hint at deep and life-giving truth. It is also unscriptural, in a way that leaves children in a double bind. On the one hand, it encourages false hopes for children who are experiencing loss or grief: it suggests that God will act for us, as he is seen to have done for the disciples, by magically removing the pain, turning back the clock, making everything okay again. On the other hand, by establishing such false hopes, it misses the real point of Jesus' victory over death. For we find that God does not, in fact, "bring back" those we love, as he "brought back" Jesus. So instead we are left in the odd position of coming to church at Easter to rejoice, because some grown-ups long ago and far away got back their dead friend and were able to dry their tears and smile again. We may be sincerely and generously glad for *them*, but how is this good news for *us*? Why should this one happy ending somehow convince us that love is always stronger than death?

Any story with a happy ending imparts hope, to some degree, to its hearers. But even the smallest child in the church is likely to sense that the Easter story is not just one story among many, but is somehow *the* story—that the hope it imparts is our central, crucial, identifying hope. By that token, its happy ending should be the happiest, most solid, satisfyingly cosmic "happily ever after" anywhere. But it isn't. Jesus comes back, but he doesn't really come back. He comes back in a puzzling, mysterious way, and then, shortly afterward, goes away again. The disciples don't get what they were hoping for. The happy ending, in fact, lies outside this narrative: like the risen Lord himself, it isn't where we are looking for it.

The truth of the Easter story is more subtle, more complex, harder to put into words but on a wordless level deeply satisfying. Jesus has not "come back." He has not been *restored to life*, as were those whom he himself brought back from the dead during his earthly ministry (Lazarus, Jairus' daughter, the widow's son), who returned to their families to live out the remainder of a natural life span, still subject to natural death. The Scriptures are very clear that this is not at all what we mean by the resurrection of Jesus.

His resurrection is indeed a restoration from death to life. But the quality of that life is so different from before that the Scriptures are driven to describe it in phrases like "the first-begotten of the dead," and "a new creation." His friends have met him again, not as the friend and teacher they knew and loved, but as a mysterious and unclassifiable human presence, known more surely in the Word of God and the Breaking of Bread than in the old familiar face, voice, and mannerisms. The clock has not turned back. Rather, they (and we) are pushed forward, with dizzying suddenness, onto a whole new road: we are to follow our Master who has passed through the grave and gate of death into the new life of the kingdom, and who asks us to join him in offering that life to every-one—*whether or not they ever knew and loved him as he was before.*

The Gospel of John uses a simpler, very revealing terminology. It merely refers to Jesus, as he goes to the cross, as being *glorified.* The whole of Christ's saving work—Gethsemane, cross, descent to the dead, resurrection, and ascension—is taken up under this one terminology. When Jesus is glorified—when he has died and risen, and become our forerunner in a new kind of life with God—he withdraws, after a few weeks, from physical presence in our local space and time. This does not mean that his new life is merely "spiritual," that in fact, all Jesus has done in rising from the dead is "die and go to heaven." The Scriptures insist that his risen body is physical—it can be touched, it can eat. But its physical properties are new and unprecedented, and its proper place, ultimately, is not in one identifiable space and time but at the right hand of the Fa-ther. Christ comes back from the dead to offer us not happiness and fun, but eternal joy. In taking a risen and glorified but still physical human nature into a place beyond space and time, Jesus breaks down once and for all the barrier between Creator and crea-tion, which he first breached in becoming incarnate among us. He brings all of us, and all of nature, home to God, where the true "happily ever after" ending will be found, farther off than we thought at first, but much more glorious, more solemn, and more joyous.

The accounts of the post-resurrection appearances in the gos-pels, for all their poignancy and power, do no more than sketch the bare outline of the paschal mystery. They offer the raw data. The earth-shaking implications are worked out elsewhere in the Scriptures, and many of them may be surprising and even repel-lent to us at first, with our culturally based preconceptions about happy reunions between loving friends and souls going to heaven, free at last from the encumbrance of the body.

It takes us, in church, fifty days just to scratch the surface of this mystery. In the Great Fifty Days, we cross the bridge from gospel to church, from knowing Jesus as friend, teacher, and wonder-worker to knowing him as indwelling Spirit and Lord of all. The apostles themselves had to cross this bridge: the story of the ascension is simply the final stage of a movement in which Jesus is always slipping through their fingers as they try to hold him to the familiar patterns they knew before. We are being quite false to history if we give children, or ourselves, the idea that knowing the risen Lord consists of holding steadily before our imaginations the happiness of his friends when he (so tantalizingly, so temporarily) came back to them.

By the same token, we are making a mistake if we convey the notion that knowing Jesus in the church means, in general, a steady task of projecting ourselves into an imagined world of the gospels. Saying "Jesus is my friend" may seem to oblige us to (in effect) pretend to be one of the people who knew Jesus intimately as he was before the crucifixion, or to imagine ourselves encountering him in our lives today in the same way as did the many characters who fill the pages of the gospels, who brought him their troubles and received immediate and obvious help.

Children love to project themselves into stories, and the Scriptures for the Great Fifty Days of Easter show us how very much more there is to the story than first meets the eye. The lectionary in this season holds before us some of the richest and best of scriptural images: shepherd and lamb, vine and mansion, holy people, royal priesthood, City of God, river of life, union with Christ through baptism into his death, as well as the familiar stories of a community of everyday people lit up from within by the light of their personal experience of the risen Lord.

We can know Jesus—the *risen and eternal Lord*—in a multitude of different and equally valid ways. One of these is of course our projection of ourselves into the gospel story. Another, thankfully much more available to children today than formerly, is our awareness of a deep and indefinable *solemn joy* as we kneel among our sisters and brothers to receive a morsel of bread, a sip of wine. Yet another is our yearning for the City of God, where all losses are indeed restored and all tears are dried—where the happy ending finally and fully arrives, with a wedding and a feast and everybody truly living happily ever after.

# NOTES

1. Walter Wangerin, *The Glory Story* (St. Louis: Concordia, Arch Books, 1974).

# Chapter 9

# "Now Say You're Sorry"

THERE IS A STANDARD little script that we use when we need to patch up a quarrel, or repair a strained relationship, or smooth over a bumpy moment. One person says, "I'm sorry." The other one says, "That's okay." As soon as our children can talk, we teach them this script. Prying apart two screaming toddlers, we stand them in front of us, and when we have finished reading them a catalog of their crimes, we tell them, "Now say you're sorry." Children learn that the phrase "I'm sorry," along with "please" and "thank you," is one of the "magic words" that adults expect in certain circumstances.

By the time we have become adults, more or less adept at polite social interactions, we have learned to use the phrase "I'm sorry" in all kinds of contexts:

> "I'm sorry you have a cold."
> "I'm sorry your car was stolen."
> "I'm sorry I bumped into you when I opened the door too suddenly."
> "I'm sorry I never wrote to you the way I promised."
> "I'm sorry I lied to you about where I was going after work."
> "I'm sorry I took the money from the pension fund."

Real confusion arises when it is unclear which sense of "sorry" is at work. When we simply say, "I'm sorry I hurt you," neither we nor the person we have hurt may have a clear idea whether we are accepting blame and expressing repentance, or asking to be excused for an honest mistake, or merely expressing regret for something that just "happened." And the reply, "That's okay," may mean simply "No big deal, no problem," or it may be the sign of a serious, costly, reconciliation—saying, in effect: "Now that you have admitted that what you did was hurtful, we are no longer alienated from each other. We can put it behind us and begin again."

The language we use to talk about wrongdoing is as fuzzy as the language we use to express apology and regret. The word "wrong" can refer to simple mistakes, such as "the wrong answer." It can also mean "morally bad" or "evil," in expressions such as "I did wrong," or "It was wrong to take the tape player from the store without paying for it." This fuzziness of so much of our language encourages lifelong confusion about sin and forgiveness. Starting as children, we easily pick up the idea that not only "doing wrong" but also "getting something wrong" is a sin—that anything that makes us feel small and ugly and stupid, any kind of "messing up," is shameful and sinful and needs to be apologized for and forgiven.

Children are inexperienced, awkward, and unskilled. They are eager to gain mastery of themselves, to learn skills and graces; they feel keenly how much adult approval rides on their progress. As we teach and admonish children, we may give them the idea that the mistakes they inevitably make as they learn and grow are what we mean by "sin"—particularly the kind of mistakes that involve getting on the nerves of adults, or failing to read their minds or to offer them the ego gratification they are seeking from their children.

Now, as a parent, I can see this from both sides. I can make my children feel like rotten human beings for needing help with a project when I am busy and preoccupied, for example, or for making noise when I have a headache, or leaving toys lying around, or forgetting a hat or jacket at school. And we can make children feel guilty and ashamed for an inability to master academic or athletic skills, to spell or draw or play the piano or catch a ball or tie their shoes.

Many Sunday school and worship materials for children actually promote this confusion. In an effort to use familiar, mild, and non-threatening language in helping children ask God's forgiveness, they will say things like, "God forgives us when we do something wrong," or "God forgives us when we forget to be loving," or "Dear God, we are sorry for our mistakes." All of this language encourages children to believe that "messing up" is itself a sin. But that is not what Scripture means by sin.

In the letter to the Ephesians, sin is described as "hardness of heart." Hardness of heart is what makes us able to say to ourselves, as we are about to do something we know is wrong, "I don't care. I'm going to do it anyway." Hardness of heart is what makes us able to say to ourselves, when there is something we know we should be doing, "I don't care. I'll do it later. I'm not in the mood for that right now."

Hardness of heart builds around each one of us a wall of unseeing, uncaring indifference toward all that might change us, all that might spur us to action, all that might open us up and make us tender and vulnerable, all that might force us to regard other people, and the world itself, as real and important. From our earliest years this tendency exists in us right alongside the potential to be fully alive, caring, whole human beings. Children know it well: it's behind laziness, tantrums, grabbing, cruelty, and most casually destructive behavior. Carelessness, or what the medieval moralists called the sin of "sloth," is every bit as central to our brokenness, and as hard to overcome, as the more glamorous sins of pride and greed and lust. Its basic line, "Who cares?" is what sets us up for almost any kind of abuse of others, of the creation, of ourselves, and especially those over whom we have power.

At our baptism we promise to "renounce" Satan—that is, to call sin by the same name God calls it, instead of the various names by which it is glossed over, glamorized, or obfuscated by the Father of Lies. We are not promising that we will be stronger than "the law of sin which dwells in our members," the hard-heartedness that causes us all, again and again, to choose what we know is hateful and hurtful. What we are promising is that when we "come to ourselves," like the Prodigal Son in the pigpen, we will be speaking the same language as God, and therefore be capable of accepting his forgiveness, and putting on the new clothes with gladness.

Weakness, fallibility, and forgetfulness are not sins. Mistakes are not sins; equally, sins are not mistakes. There are plenty of adults who have taught themselves to think of all offenses as mere trivial accidents—as things that "just happened," unrelated to their own powers to see the consequences and to choose. Partly in reaction to the heavy load of guilt that many of us felt in childhood, for things that were not our fault, we now try so hard to "feel good about ourselves" that we expect to be excused for whatever we do, simply as a matter of entitlement and routine. When we do commit a real offense, we are baffled and upset by the difficulty others have in excusing us as we expect to be excused, "now that I've said I'm sorry."

"God loves turkeys" is not the gospel. It is far more than our bumbling weakness that Jesus died to overcome; and he has a more radical agenda in mind for us than merely repairing our self-esteem without changing our behavior.

It is easy to celebrate Jesus' forgiveness and grace if we imagine all its recipients as ordinary nice people who have somehow blown it, or have been dropped from the mainstream, misunderstood, or left out. It is easy to imagine we have learned to repent—or to forgive—when all we have actually learned to do is gloss over or excuse minor injuries, failures, or misunderstandings. It is easy to confuse indifference with charity, to imagine ourselves as peacemakers when we have never known what it is to hate and fear a genuine enemy, or had to live with the lasting effects of an injury or loss brought on by someone else's vindictiveness, casual negligence, or unscrupulousness. It is easy to suggest to children that all we have to do is "be nice" and "love other people" and learn to get along with others, and somehow keep from "messing up," and the problem of sin will shrivel to manageable proportions. It won't.

Real forgiveness of real injuries is not easy. It can only happen when both parties remain in relationship, and when the one who has caused the injuries says "I'm sorry" in a way that clearly means, not "Isn't it too bad that these things happened," or "There, now I've said it; I hope you're satisfied; now can I get on with my life?" but, "I understand that what I did was destructive, and that I knew it was destructive and did it anyway. I will not try to excuse it, and I do not intend to do it again. Can you now, simply out of love, set it aside and rebuild our relationship?" When the Scriptures repeatedly insist on our need to confess our sins to God and express true repentance, this is not some kind of power trip on God's part, requiring that we grovel before him and mumble certain magic words before we can be restored to favor. It is simply an acknowledgement that even the Almighty cannot remain in relationship with those who continue to be hard-hearted and will not call what they have done by its real name, acknowledge its destructiveness, and show themselves willing to change—whether or not they are confident that they are able to change.

We need to remind ourselves and our children again and again that adults, for all their competence and power, for all their apparent immunity to criticism, sin just as much as—no, much more than—children. I vividly remember as a child being firmly convinced that the Prayer Book phrase, "tied and bound with the chain of our sins," referred in my case to my complete inability to say the right thing that would avoid hurting the grown-ups' feelings when they were tense or distracted. The adults were, probably, dimly aware that they were being unfair to me, but did not feel like bothering to overcome their crabbiness. Now that I am a parent, I see the same abuse of power, the same hardness of heart, in myself. But it is the child—who is trying so hard to be "good"—who feels guilty.

# Chapter 10

# Pew Art

A S  A N  U N D E R G R A D U A T E  at Bryn
Mawr, I used to knit in class. I was not the only
one who did. It was a women's college, and such
behavior was accepted as normal, though it was an
unwritten rule that anyone who used metal needles had better be
sure never to let them drop through the stitches to the floor. When
I came to Yale for graduate work, I discovered that *no one* knitted
in class. This was 1972, and though the graduate school had been
coeducational for years, I was reluctant to tarnish the image of the
serious-minded woman scholar by pioneering in this particular
way. I left my knitting at home. I wish I hadn't. Oral reports were
the mainstay of the graduate seminar and when they were boring
or ran way overtime (as they usually did), I found myself resenting
this appalling waste of time far more than I would have if I'd had
my knitting along—then at least I would have had something to
show for the afternoon's activities. But more important, I found
that I was attending far less alertly even to exciting and interesting
material.

Without the knitting to occupy my hands and the right side of
my brain, I stared out the window, I daydreamed, I grew sleepy.
Now, whenever I think I can do it without grave discourtesy, I
bring my knitting to meetings, workshops, lectures, conferences.
Knitting *helps me to listen*, by giving a simple occupation to the

parts of my body—eyes and hands—that would otherwise distract my brain from its job of attending to what I am hearing.

It takes work to attend to the linear, verbal, left-brain material that we must assimilate if we are to learn from a lecture, a seminar, an oral presentation, or a sermon. For most of us (and probably for nearly all children, especially in the age of television), it takes less work to assimilate visual, non-verbal material, and if the eyes are free to wander, the brain follows, becomes fully engaged in processing the wealth of images it encounters, and stops bothering to attend to the more difficult verbal material. But if the eyes are focused on a simple task, using the hands, it seems that enough of the brain is left free to attend to the spoken word.

I don't have the nerve to suggest that adults be encouraged to knit in church—though I've sat through many a sermon that made me wish I had that knitting along. But what about encouraging children to draw in church? Many of them will do it anyway, as we all know. In their book, *Going to Church with Children*, Stan Stewart, Pauline Stewart, and Richard Green describe a common situation:

> A friend was sitting beside a small girl who was attending worship with her mother. During the sermon the small girl took a stewardship envelope and drew upon it. The mother who was engrossed with the sermon did not notice what her daughter was doing. During the last hymn, the mother caught a glimpse of her daughter's handiwork on the back of the envelope. Without looking at it, she reprimanded her daughter for drawing in church. "You should have been paying attention," she growled as she hurried her daughter out of the pew. The piece of art was left crumpled on the seat. My friend uncrumpled it. The small girl had drawn a decorated heart shape. Inside its borders she had written, "Jesus loves me."

Providing plain paper and a (limited) number of crayons or markers not only saves pew cards and pledge envelopes. It also helps our children to listen. The drawings they make may be a form of meditation or even of prayer:

> Recently I had the privilege of taking an eleven-year-old child to worship. This girl had never before been into a church. During the sermon, I silently gave to her a piece of paper and a pen.

She occupied herself with drawing for ten minutes or so. After the service I was able to study her art. She had drawn two scenes. The first was a picture of a woman dressed as a bride. I knew that the girl's mother had deserted her children when my young friend was only three years old. The second picture was a sketch of the inside of the church. Prominent in the picture was the cross. Below it stood a figure behind the pulpit. I do not know what is the exact meaning these images had to my young friend, but I know that thinking on these things during a worship service was a most suitable way to use her time.[1]

On Good Shepherd Sunday several years ago, our family was in Washington, D.C., visiting my parents. We took our children, then ten and almost seven, to Washington Cathedral. The space, the music, the movement, and the stained glass were impressive, but when the sermon began, our younger daughter began to squirm and complain. The preacher had a British accent, and his words, distorted by the sound system and echoing through the vast nave, were very hard to hear. No wonder she was getting bored— but all the more important that she should not disturb others who were straining to catch the sermon. In desperation, I gave her the bulletin and a ballpoint pen, and suggested that she draw the Good Shepherd. She went instantly to work, and filled two bulletins, drawing not only the Good Shepherd, but also the eucharist; a bride-and-groom scene where the groom is labeled "Jesus" and the bride "us"; two visions of the New Jerusalem; a flying bird; a crowned heart labeled "God"; a running horse; and rows and rows of hearts. The sermon, now that we could hear it, was a simple and eloquent act of evangelism, describing, for the many unchurched people who were visiting the cathedral, some of what it means to take part in Christian community. Nearly every one of Margaret's drawings was in keeping with this theme. Her mind had been freed to listen.

"Pew art," as Stewart, Stewart, and Green call it, is "seldom a random selection of scribbles." Its most common subjects are hearts, crosses, and manger scenes. These are, in fact, almost the only Christian images available to either children or adults in our culture—but they are only the tip of the iceberg of the imagery available in Scripture and Christian tradition.

One of the functions of Scripture is to give us a vocabulary of canonical images through which to focus the vague blur of our own spirituality. Long ago the church undertook to arrange and pattern the scriptural story: the church tells the story bit by bit in the lectionary over the course of the year, and briefly recapitulates it in every Eucharistic Prayer. At such occasions as the Service of Lessons and Carols at Christmas or the Great Vigil of Easter, the church goes to great lengths to underline the story's very highest points, to remind us of its basic shape: creation, alienation, redemption, exile, death, and rebirth. In placing side by side each week a Hebrew Scripture, a psalm, an epistle, and a gospel, the church sets the Scriptures into dialogue with each other. We begin to see that the story of the chosen people, the story of the Son of God, the story of the church, and the story of each one of us, are one story, which in turn is interwoven with the seasons of nature and the cycle of every human life.

Certain powerful images occur again and again, in ever-expanding contexts: water, wind, fire; light, darkness; flood, rainbow, altar; exile, pilgrimage, return, homecoming, feast; river, tree, well, rock, desert, tent, mountain, garden, city, temple; seed, grain, vineyard, winepress, bread, wine, blood, oil, salt; shepherd, lamb, dove; king, priest, judge, master; father, mother, child, bride, bridegroom; crowns, robes, palms, jewels. But we do little in Sunday school and adult education to reinforce our perception of the story through visual means. And in comparison with our verbal liturgical arts, our visual liturgical arts are impoverished indeed: Protestant culture since the sixteenth century has narrowed down the range of accessible, recognizable scriptural images to little more than these three: the cross, the manger scene, and the idea of love, which in America today means, of course, the heart.

Children draw what they are thinking about. But it would seem that children, without help, do not draw what they hear; they draw what they have seen. They develop a repertoire of visual clichés that they refine and repeat endlessly, and through which they seek to order and understand their world.[2] The obvious inference is that whatever we help them to *see* and to *draw*, we are also helping them to think about and to understand, to remember, recognize, and work with: we are providing them with tools for theological thought, for devotion, prayer, and, ultimately, moral choice and personal growth.

Margaret has grown up in a household where imaging the Scriptures is a matter of daily interest and conversation, and in a Sunday School where children paint murals, make banners, dramatize the Festival of Lessons and Carols and the Easter Vigil, and play constantly with visual and hands-on materials representing the rich and varied images of Scripture. Her drawings on that morning at Washington Cathedral show a sensitive response not only to the subject of the sermon but also to the printed material in the bulletin she was decorating. For instance, her images of the New Jerusalem adorn the text of the offertory anthem, which included the lines, "Rise, Sion, rise! and looking forth, Behold thy children round thee!" Her drawings employ a vocabulary of scriptural images that is much larger than the standard trio of hearts, crosses, and manger scenes. She has combined these images in original and intriguing ways; she has been given the tools to make the Scriptures and the liturgy her own.

We can and must do much more to offer our children the nourishment of a rich variety of scriptural images. In the midst of a culture bloated on junk food, the church has offered its children only crumbs.

# Notes

1. *Going to Church with Children* (Melbourne, Australia: Joint Board of Christian Education, 1987), pp. 60-61.

2. See Betty Edwards, *Drawing on the Right Side of the Brain* (New York: St. Martin's Press, 1979), chapter 5.

# PART THREE

# Celebrating Together With Children

Chapter 11

# Learning Through Celebration

CHILDREN ARE DEEPLY liturgical beings. They show this in their eager, wholehearted enjoyment of holidays—not only as occasions for fun and food but also as celebrations of particular themes, ideas, events, and memories. For most children in our culture, the liturgical year is one that has been developed by the elementary school teachers and the greeting card companies, in which there is a celebration and a focus for each month from September through June—the new school year for September, Halloween for October, Thanksgiving for November, Christmas/Hanukkah for December, New Year's and Martin Luther King for January, Valentine's Day for February, St. Patrick's Day for March, Easter/Passover for April, Mother's Day for May, Father's Day and graduation for June—and a host of patriotic commemorations, mostly focusing on past wars, scattered throughout the year. Some of these holidays and seasonal focuses provide legitimate curricular structure or speak with genuine mythic power to children's emotional needs; others clearly exist only to provide a theme for classroom decorations and a reason for selling cards and novelties.

There is no coherent story that is told, cumulatively, by the whole year; for each holiday or season we pick up and then put down one or two fragments of our national and cultural consciousness. And the arbitrariness of the standard series of celebrations has encouraged a trend that was already present in the greeting card industry. Whatever the source of the holiday, whatever its original focus, once it finds its way into the mainstream culture its message becomes simply, "Have a happy day." To be sure, each of the holidays has its standard colors and images, but as far as Hallmark Cards are concerned, the only agenda for any of them is that we have a happy time. Even Valentines for children rarely end with the traditional message, "I love you," or "Be my valentine." They say, "Happy Valentine's Day."

Children, however, know perfectly well that Halloween is not just about autumn and pumpkins, but about spooks, skeletons, and terror; that the secular Christmas is not just about Frosty the Snowman, but about the deeply serious question of whether Santa Claus knows and loves each of us enough to visit us with gifts even if we are small, insignificant, and sometimes naughty. It is not the fault of children in our culture that they are left to explore such issues through the increasingly murky glass of our secular celebrations, instead of being invited to experience them so much more deeply and authentically in genuinely traditional festivals—or, better yet, in the rich and varied rhythm of the Christian year.

The church's year, with its lucid yet subtle arrangement of fasts and feasts, of penitence, preparation, and praise, its synthesis of Scripture and salvation history with the life of Jesus, our own lives, and the rhythms of the natural seasons, can provide a backdrop of extraordinary richness for children's spiritual and emotional lives— as it does, of course, for many adults. And yet it has been terribly underused by those who teach and write for children in the church, and by Christian families. The recent trends toward using the lectionary as the framework for Sunday school curriculums, and toward having children present for the entire eucharistic liturgy, week by week, suggest that the church's year may be in the process of being rediscovered as resources for catechesis and children's spiritual growth. But there is a long way to go.

Minorities are well aware of the need to cultivate traditions and rituals and to transmit them, deliberately and consciously, to the next generation. Jews in the United States, for example, devote much of their energy in religious education, both at home and in the congregation, to passing on to their children a broad and deep store of tradition by means of holidays and other celebrations. Even in secular libraries and bookstores one can find an abundant supply of colorful books for Jewish children of all ages, covering the whole spectrum of the Jewish liturgical year and the Jewish life cycle. Comparable materials on Christian celebrations simply do not exist.

For generations, it seems, religious educators and religious writers for Christian children in the English-speaking world have by their own choice limited themselves to just a few themes: Bible stories, prayers, and moral issues. Our writing and programming for children still overwhelmingly reflect a tradition that treats faith as essentially a personal, private matter, and trusts to the mainstream culture to provide whatever communal reinforcement is needed. For the last several generations, that trust has been increasingly misplaced.

In the age of inclusiveness and pluralism, the schools and the media are allowed, and even encouraged, to celebrate the distinctive features (including the actual beliefs) of any and all minority identifications. But any presentation of the specific religious content of the majority culture, as opposed to its shallowest and blandest pieties and clichés, risks being perceived, however implausibly, as cultural imperialism or proselytism—as an attempt to impose a "normal," "majority" practice or point of view. The public school will no longer teach our children traditional Christmas carols, but it will go right on teaching them "Rudolph the Red-Nosed Reindeer" and "Winter Wonderland"—and maybe even a genuine Hebrew Hanukkah song.

If we want Christian celebration and Christian community to mean anything to our children, we will have to teach them ourselves. Adult members of the liturgical churches are well aware how the weekly and seasonal liturgical structures help us organize the huge mass of scriptural material, doctrine, and the rhythm of daily and yearly life into patterns that are aesthetically and psychologically accessible, rich, challenging, and satisfying. Yet we have somehow expected children to do this for themselves, with no more resources than a brief exposure to dozens of unconnected fragments of Scripture (drawn strictly from the kiddie canon, and usually rewritten in the mode of "David and Rebecca meet Jesus in Capernaum and it changes their life"), a small repertoire of doctrinally skimpy prayers and songs, and an immense literature of moral-dilemmas-in-everyday-life, that bind heavy burdens on children's shoulders and offer them precious little gospel faith or hope.

When we finally do get around to calling their attention to the church's year, its sacraments, and its life-cycle celebrations, we put our efforts into learning *about* these things, rather than inviting children to experience them, in spirit and in truth. Often, we package such learning as arcane lore, to be learned by rote (the colors of the liturgical seasons, the names of the priest's vestments and the altar vessels), as if our only reason for transmitting this piece of tradition were to raise up a new generation of altar guild leaders.

But the way to learn about a feast is to *celebrate* it—preferably from the earliest possible age, as the Jews (once again) can show us. The Jewish tradition has centered its festivals in the home, where the generations are forced to discover ways of celebrating together, rather than in the congregation, where children can be sequestered away in a classroom. When celebration is alive and well, the feast itself is the teaching tool. The melodies of certain hymns, the smells of certain holiday foods, the very look of the sky and feel of the air at a particular time of the year, can set off a whole train of associations, memories, and emotions in us. We re-experience the feast and all it stands for, with our whole selves, in all its richness.

While the progress of the Jewish calendar is from festival to festival, that of the Christian one, at least in its present-day Anglican form, is from season to season, with Christmas, Easter, and to a much lesser degree Epiphany and Pentecost, as the high points that provide climaxes and transitions. Perhaps this perception of the liturgical year as background rather than as primary action is part of why we have failed to realize its potential in Christian nurture: seasonal themes are simply less exciting than celebrations that focus on a single, climactic day or event, and so, once again, we have found that all roads lead to Christmas and Easter. But there are at least two other possible ways of looking at the year, to supply it with more highlighted moments among the bars of color that represent the seasons.

The first is the medieval cycle of fixed holy days and saints' days, each with its agricultural and social traditions, which still offers some fine opportunities for meaningful parish celebrations. Michaelmas, St. Francis' Day, Candlemas, Annunciation, the Rogation Days, and especially Corpus Christi, as well as a parish's own patronal festival, have real possibilities. St. Francis' and Rogation Day could both be used as ways of working with the doctrine of creation, a topic that is of vital importance in an age of environmental crisis, and one that has lost ground liturgically since Morning Prayer (with its canticles of praise for creation) ceased to be a primary form of Sunday morning worship.

The second way of looking at the year is provided by the Prayer Book's designation of certain occasions as baptismal feasts. All Saints' Day, the Feast of the Baptism of our Lord, the Great Vigil of Easter, and Pentecost punctuate the parish year at approximately equal intervals, and their association with baptism allows each one to be pegged firmly to the main structure of salvation history without losing its individual emphasis on a certain aspect of that story. Celebrating these feasts with an eye to highlighting their baptismal elements means that we can activate in them many levels of significance at once—Scripture, salvation history, sacrament, individual faith journey, personal commitment, ethical implications, Christian community. As we do this repeatedly in the course of the year, each time from the vantage point of a different feast, we begin to create a kaleidoscopic experience of what it means to believe the gospel and to be a Christian in community that is far more likely to have a deep and lasting impact on children than any classroom lesson.

Holidays that really matter in a human community take time and effort to celebrate. There is a period of anticipation and preparation, then the festival itself, which dominates, at the very least, one whole morning or one whole afternoon or evening. Finally, there are the memories, which gather up and merge the celebrations from many different years; for children, there is also the work of anticipating the next celebration, when each of us will be a year older and have a slightly different, and bigger, part to play. And as the year rolls round and the next repetition begins to draw near, there is the delightful job of clueing in newcomers and younger children whose memories are unclear: whetting their appetites, teasing them, saying, "Wait till you see what happens after *that!*" and "You're not old enough to do such-and-such yet, but when you're as old as me..." Celebration, in other words, is *liturgy:* when it is working well, its strength lies in its annual repetition, with few novelties. Liturgy is very hard work to develop from scratch. It is less hard to perpetuate, though the scale and level of detail it requires mean that the labor and love involved are never trivial.

The cycle of celebrations with which we now mark the children's year in our congregation evolved slowly and continues to change gradually with the changing face of the parish and the changing needs of the children. The first to be developed were the Christmas pageant[1] and Palm Saturday, to fill in the liturgical dimension of Christmas and to provide for Holy Week and Easter some of the necessary emphasis to convey their importance in the year, especially as compared with Christmas. Next came All Saints' Saturday, then the Easter pageant[2] (which is presented only every two or three years, rather than annually like the Christmas pageant). The year was rounded out with Corpus Christi Saturday, which we have found to be a far more fertile early-summer theme than Pentecost, and which balances, with its eucharistic focus, the baptismal emphasis of the other celebrations. (Once, when within

the space of five weeks in May and June two couples chose to celebrate their weddings on Sunday morning, we managed to draw
themes for Christian marriage out of Corpus Christi as well.)
Three Kings' Saturday has been celebrated only once, as a primarily pre-baptismal rather than seasonal celebration.

As an inner-city parish, we have had a number of occasions to
baptize children from severely dysfunctional and unsupportive
families, who have been coming to church of their own free choice
and who are looking to the parish to provide them with a community to belong to. The Sunday school and its teachers function as
sponsoring community, and the pre-baptismal preparation is done
in that context, as celebration rather than as academic work. In fact
the academic model is found almost nowhere in our Sunday
school, whose name is therefore doubly misleading, since its main
work no longer happens on Sundays.

On Sunday mornings we have at most about forty minutes before we are called into church for communion. We spend at least
half of it in worship, and the other half responding to the Scripture that was presented in worship—that is, we are offering the Liturgy of the Word at our own several age levels. It is in the
Saturdays and the pageants, however, that we really have time to
work with the gospel, and to mark the passing of the church's year
in ways that will be stirring, exciting, and memorable to children—
as the church's worship itself is stirring, exciting, and memorable
when it responds to the gospel in spirit and in truth. Then, for our
children, the changing seasons will carry with them a store of
memories that grows and deepens year by year, to provide rich and
challenging intuitions of the ways of our God among us—past, present, and future. And by their fruits you shall know them.

# NOTES

1. See my book *Go, Tell It on the Mountain* (New Haven: The Sunday Paper,
1985).

2. For the Easter pageant and detailed descriptions of Palm Saturday activities, see my *Risen With Christ: Celebrating the Paschal Mystery in the Parish Family* (New Haven: The Sunday Paper, 1988).

# Chapter 12

# Bathrobe Drama

THE CHRISTMAS PAGEANT is a hallowed piece of American folk culture and the subject of a wealth of affectionately condescending jokes and clichés. Think of the *Doonesbury* series, years ago, where the "fighting young priest who talks to the young" marshalls his cast of college students and ghetto youth to present a "Christmas rock-pageant" in which the part of Baby Jesus is played by a hidden forty-watt light bulb—or *The Best Christmas Pageant Ever*, poking fun at the intrepid Sunday school battle-axe who every year browbeats the same kids into playing the same roles with the same predictable prissy boredom, until the year when five young hoodlums from the wrong side of the tracks grab all the parts and propel the story to its inevitable heartwarming conclusion.

Then there are all the Christmas cards that show little kids in ill-fitting bathrobes, with sneakers peeking out from below the hems and halos slipping off their heads, gathering piously around the manger with the baby doll in it. And the ads for pageant scripts that start to arrive in the Sunday school director's mail early in the fall. So many of them are variations on the theme of "The Littlest Angel" or "The Little Drummer Boy": a lost and lonely angel, or star, or shepherd boy, or baby camel, or donkey, feels left out and worthless until, through an encounter with the newborn Christ Child, his self-esteem is wondrously restored and the whole world flooded with radiant blessing.

It's all as hokey and predictable as the TV specials about Rudolph and Charlie Brown and Scrooge and the Grinch. It's no wonder that the Christian education director feels a certain added embarrassment and social reticence as December approaches. It's hard enough at any time of year, explaining to someone at a party that one "teaches Sunday school" and dealing with the weak "Oh, that's nice" that inevitably follows. But at Christmas, weighed down by sheep costumes and carol music, rehearsal schedules and worries about flu epidemics, it's hard to persist in believing that the Christmas pageant can, and should, be a powerful piece of liturgical drama and a profoundly formative experience for the children who take part in it.

The Christmas pageant is a sentimental cliché because that is what our culture has made of Christmas. Popular Christmas stories commonly present an implied theology consisting of "redemption by babyhood," or, even more frequently, "redemption by giving." The simple presence of a wondrous infant, or a single act of kindness by a previously sour and alienated character, are seen as being sufficient to transform the world. And of course there is much emotional truth in such stories, or they would not have the appeal that they do. But they are not the gospel. They are not the Christmas story.

Simple nativity stories present only the Good News of the baby's birth (with, perhaps, an unsympathetic innkeeper and a King Herod to serve as "bad guys"). They do little to challenge children to wonder why this birth is so long awaited and so joyfully hailed. And the fictionalized dramas that tell of the redemption of a lost, lonely, sour, or misunderstood individual reinforce our current trend toward an excessively therapeutic focus in evangelism and catechesis by suggesting that Christ came to rescue maladjusted individuals and to restore the self-esteem of the picked-on— and is magically able to do so, even in the cradle. Children inevitably personalize such messages, with highly unpredictable results. I feel it is far more truthful, as liturgy, as drama, and as evangelism, to take a cue from the traditional order for the Festival of Lessons and Carols, which always begins with the reading of the story of Adam and Eve in Genesis 3. Beginning the pageant with this ancient and powerful myth forcibly reminds us that *all* people—boys and girls, adults and children, "smart" and "dumb," "popular" and "left out"—are alienated from God; all are in desperate need of a gracious Savior. This message is far too rarely told to children today.

For the last seven years our parish has presented a Christmas pageant with nine lessons and carols and the eucharist, based on the Advent and Christmas Festival of Lessons and Music in *The Book of Occasional Services*. Adults and children present the drama together, further emphasizing the universality of the Christmas message: it is not a children's story that the children dutifully absorb from adults, or a cute or pretty fable that they present for the adults' approval, but a crucial liturgical drama, in which the people of God—from kindergartners to the rector—work together to tell the central story that gives meaning to our life as a people. Children read the lessons and appear as Adam and Eve, Mary and Joseph; children and adults together sing the carols and play the shepherds, angels, and animals. The children write the prayers of the people, the Great Thanksgiving, and the postcommunion prayer, and, at the offertory, dress the altar and vest the priest.

The drama begins with Adam and Eve, two pre-teenagers in tan leotards and tights, taking the fruit of the forbidden tree. They then must run guiltily and hide from the Angel of the Lord (a lay person, dressed in alb and white chasuble), who calls them out from their hiding place to confess their transgression and go weeping down the center aisle to the back of the church, as the congregation sings "Savior of the Nations, Come." Adam and Eve remain in their exile as the Advent wreath is lit and a procession enters, accompanying the prophecy from Isaiah, "There shall come forth a shoot from the stump of Jesse, and a branch shall grow out of his roots....The wolf shall dwell with the lamb...for the earth shall be full of the knowledge of the Lord as the waters cover the sea."

In the third lesson, we see God's gracious purpose for all of us, in the words of the apocryphal book of Baruch: "Take off the garment of your sorrow and affliction, O Jerusalem, and put on for ever the beauty of the glory from God...." Adam and Eve, still in their leotards and fig leaves, come forward and stand before the Angel of the Lord, who clothes them in albs and golden chasubles and crowns their heads with gold crowns: "Arise, O Jerusalem, stand upon the height and look toward the east, and see your children gathered from west to east, at the word of the Holy One, rejoicing that God has remembered them."

Thereafter Adam and Eve stand with the angels as the pageant continues with the annunciation, the birth of Jesus, and the visit of the shepherds to the manger. Finally, after communion and the closing hymn, the Angel of the Lord stands alone by the tree that has already changed from the forbidden tree to the tree of Jesse and now becomes the tree of life. The Angel reads from the Book of Revelation: "I am the Alpha and the Omega, the first and the last....Blessed are those who wash their robes, that they may have the right to the tree of life....He who testifies to these things says, 'Surely I am coming soon.'" And the congregation replies, "Amen. Come, Lord Jesus!"

Seven years with this script has done nothing to wear it thin; on the contrary, children look forward to it from year to year, remember its high points, and, gradually, learn its Scriptures by heart, accompanied by vivid images of the enacted story. I have many memories of the way the pageant has challenged particular children to confront the meaning of the Incarnation and the gospel for their own lives; but the two I want to tell have to do with the impact of the Adam and Eve story.

Several years ago, a boy named Mark was chosen to play the part of Adam. Like most twelve-year-old boys, Mark didn't really relish the job of wearing skin-tight leotards and playing opposite a girl in similar costume, but he was a dutiful and cooperative kid and agreed to do it. He was big for his age, and bony, and when he appeared in his costume at the dress rehearsal he was clearly ill at ease, hunching his shoulders and keeping his crossed arms extended straight down across his middle. The fact that the church was freezing cold exacerbated this already tense body language. But he gamely went through with the first scene, and retreated with Eve down the center aisle.

Then came the moment in the third scene when the human pair returned to the front of the church to be welcomed and robed and crowned. As the angel pulled the alb over Mark's shoulders and its folds fell into place, his body straightened. His shoulders went back, his head up; his breathing relaxed, his expression became confident, then joyful. The gold chasuble went over the alb; then the crown was placed on his head. The transformation was complete. Warmth, certainly, but also dignity, flowed through him. I never asked him how he had felt at that moment; perhaps he himself was not even conscious of how deeply he had acted out in his body the experience of being raised from shame to honor, from disgrace to grace, from naked discomfort under the scrutiny of God and the community to the dignity of standing before God and the community clothed with honor, justified and lifted up. But what could be a more fitting image of the redemption that the Savior's coming promises to each one of us?

The other story concerns Nicole, a little girl from a troubled home. Nicole normally pays little attention in Sunday school; in fact she frequently disappears for five or ten minutes at a time, to be found in the library or under a table in a classroom. When she is present and watching the teacher, she often interrupts the lesson with loud comments, earnest but often completely irrelevant. Her drawings frequently represent people being punished by God for the bad things they do.

When the pageant was at the early rehearsal stage, the teacher was standing in front of a bulletin board with schematic drawings of the various scenes. She described the Adam and Eve scene, using the analogy, familiar to all the children, of being told, "Go to your room! And don't come out till I tell you it's time!" as a way of bringing the Scripture to life. Five minutes later, describing the lesson from Baruch, she told the children, "This is where God says to the man and the woman, 'Come out of your rooms now—I love you—I want you to be happy; I want you to be my own children forever!'" Nicole seemed to be paying no more attention than usual, but the following week, as the teacher once again stood before the bulletin board and asked, "Who remembers what happens in this scene?" Nicole jumped up in great excitement. "That's where God says, 'Go to your room!'" she announced in her most forceful voice. "And then he says, 'Come out! I love you!' And they get to be his children again, forever!"

The pageant didn't solve Nicole's problems: she still goes and hides during Sunday school, and she still draws pictures of people being punished by God. She still deals with her knowledge that her mother deserted her when she was still a toddler by sobbing silently throughout the annunciation scene every year. But that dramatic moment, when the human pair (who represent you and me, Mark and Nicole, Mommy and Daddy, priest and Sunday school teacher) stand before the Angel of the Lord to be welcomed with open arms and with crowns of glory—that moment got through to her. The language of Scripture itself was set in motion and spoke to the heart of a child.

# Chapter 13

# Palm Saturday

**H**OLY WEEK AND EASTER are the heart of the church year, but children in our culture find much more to anticipate in the coming of Christmas than they do in the coming of Easter. The secular version of the paschal feast runs a pretty poor second to the secular Christmas: candy, new clothes, egg decorating, and fuzzy animals are nice enough, but they are no match for Christmas with its gifts, decorations, piped-in carols, wall-to-wall jollity, and "holiday spirit." In comparison with Santa Claus, who at least has a certain mythic power, the Easter Bunny is a ludicrous travesty, about on a level with the Tooth Fairy in style, substance, and ability to stir children's emotions. And the church, I suspect, often provides little help in coming to see the paschal mystery as an incomparable high point in our yearly cycle.

It's hard not to buy into the values of one's surroundings. In a thousand different little ways we communicate to children that at Christmas everything changes: everything stops its normal activity and takes note of the Christians' feast. But Easter is a mere passing episode, with some pleasant traditions. It marks the arrival of spring, and the church certainly does seem to get excited about it, but it does not turn the child's own world upside down.

This is not to suggest that we try to make Easter go the way of Christmas in the sense of turning the month preceding it into a nightmare of frenetic busyness and consumerism. A priest I know used to say that it was a mercy of God that for a thousand years the western church has given too much honor to Christmas and too little to Easter, and as a result, Christmas rather than Easter has been commercialized and despoiled. This is indeed a grace at Eastertime, at least for adults: there is far less secular distraction to deal with. But Easter is a feast, and the way to learn about a feast is to celebrate it. Though it is not without cost to us as parents and teachers, we need to give our children more yearly tradition centered around the season of Holy Week and Easter.

In our parish, this has meant the care and feeding of Palm Saturday, an annual event in which we work to anticipate the whole range of the church's experience from Palm Sunday to Easter, through worship, storytelling, crafts, and whatever else comes to hand. The outline of the day is flexible year by year, but it normally contains each of these elements: *gathering, telling the story, working with the story, mirroring the story,* and *worship.*

(1) *Gathering* (thirty minutes) - Singing, stripping palms for the altar guild, browsing a book table, making Easter cards for family, friends, or parish shut-ins, are all possible activities. This is a time for occupying children who have already arrived, while making it easy for latecomers and guests to enter into the business at hand and into the community of children engaged in it.

(2) *Telling or experiencing the story* (forty-five minutes to one hour) - The telling of the passion and resurrection is the most basic act of Christian education. It is also the most basic act of Christian worship: telling and hearing this story are meant to make us stand before our God in awe, in thanksgiving, and in self-dedication. There is no more serious enterprise that we can undertake at Holy Week than the telling of this story compellingly and faithfully with our children, so that it will invite them into an encounter with the living Lord. *Compellingly:* the story must be powerfully and freely told, by a person who has thoroughly mastered its narrative outline and is able to engage an audience with a limited vocabulary and attention span. *Faithfully:* the telling must be free of sentimentality, condescension, and gimmicks. It must tell the truth. It must not undercut or contradict the scriptural story, or

eclipse it with fanciful or fictional embellishments. It must make no false promises—particularly, no promises of sudden, dramatic, and permanent improvements in a child's personal or social life as a result of accepting Jesus. It must respect the dignity of its young audience and allow them space to spin their own fantasies: it must not overwhelm them with programmed answers or invite a frivolous response. The storyteller is the weaver of a spell, not a tutor or a cheerleader.

There are many, many ways to tell a story, from simple narration or the use of puppets or flannelboard, to inviting children to interact with the storyteller through words, gestures, movement, song, or meditation. While ideas, challenges, and help are abundantly available in books and other resources, the only style that will be effective is one that comes naturally to the storyteller. More important than any innovative or creative methods of presentation is a truly intimate familiarity with the story's own narrative flow, and a thorough sympathy with its atmosphere and mood. It is better to err on the side of simplicity than to load oneself down with extra equipment or material that may fail to function as expected, distract the storyteller or the children, or simply break the spell. The description of our "prayer walk" in the chapter "Something Strange Is Happening" is only one way, uniquely adapted to our church building, of telling the story.

(3) *Working with the story* (two one-hour blocks, one in the morning and one in the afternoon, unless the afternoon is used for Easter pageant rehearsal) - This is the area in which you and the children have the most freedom. Almost any kind of craft or creative activity is appropriate, as long as it is suitable to the number and ages of your children, the space and facilities, and the abilities and interests of the adults on hand to help. You will almost certainly need to offer several activities at once, in different parts of the building: for your own sanity, you should plan on enrolling children in their activities in advance. This may be done by pre-registration, based on first and second choices expressed on the registration form; or, for a little more flexibility, children can sign up as they arrive, subject to the teacher's discretion. What does *not* work

is just to say, "Now everybody pick an activity and go to it," and turn them loose—unless you are prepared to have them all wandering from activity to activity all day. (The wandering, or "learning station," approach has its merits, but only when intentionally chosen and planned for, and only when the building layout supports it. All the stations should be in close proximity to each other, so that children are not roaming the corridors of your parish house unsupervised.)

The work should be absorbing, fun, and should avoid pre-programmed craft projects in which all the children make exactly the same thing, or have only to assemble precut materials or follow directions. The purpose of this creative work is to challenge the children to discover and express their own response to the story, either as individuals or as a group. If, on the way, they learn doctrine or lore (standard Christian symbols such as the dove, the fish, the butterfly, for example), well and good, but that is not the primary agenda. On the other hand, gentle direction from the teacher is needed to slow down the child who simply dives in and starts working with the materials, making a giraffe or dinosaur or space ship or whatever, without considering the story at all.

Craft activities, in which the children make something with their hands, have been more successful for us than those involving writing or performance. At various times we have tried poetry writing, liturgical dance, and improvisatory drama, with varying success. Perhaps the particular gifts of our teachers have something to do with it, but my guess is that these kinds of activities invade the child's privacy too much. The children have seemed unwilling to lay bare their response to the story in a medium as objective as words or as directly personal as body language, while in clay, paint, felt, and diorama they are much more open and uninhibited. An activity consisting only of singing has also met with only moderate enthusiasm, though a period of singing with the whole group may generate enthusiastic participation.

We try to offer, each year, a range of activities suggestive of each of the different episodes in the drama of Holy Week, from preparing banners for Palm Sunday and baking bread for Maundy Thursday, through making a clay sculpture of the crucifix and a diorama of the Marys at the tomb, decorating candles for baptismal candidates, and planting flowers in the church garden, right down to baking cookies for the festive Easter coffee hour, and of course the ever-popular dyeing of Easter eggs. Even though the children can and do dye and decorate eggs at home, they all want to do it on Palm Saturday too, and we usually schedule this activity for both morning and afternoon.

(4) *Mirroring the story* (about forty-minutes) - We have children bring their own lunches, and as they are finishing them, we have a quiet time with a movie or some other presentation. (If your group includes a significant number of very young or rambunctious kids, you may want to add a morning snack and some recess time for running around and letting off steam.) The "movie" can be a 16-mm film, a filmstrip, a videotape, a slide show, a sound recording, a live reading-aloud time, or even a skit, as long as it does not duplicate too much the style and substance of the storytelling earlier in the day.

This is not the occasion for one more retelling, this time on film, of the literal story of the passion. For one thing, filmed literal dramatizations of the passion are rarely effective. It is not an easy story to render with the camera under any circumstances, and movies made for Sunday school use tend to have a pedestrian, didactic intention, with very artificial dialogue and a heavy use of visuals clichés. This strikes exactly the wrong note for our purposes: it is neither suggestively symbolic nor relentlessly incarnational, but a hybrid which conveys the power of neither. Rather, our agenda here is to "mirror" the story: to expose the children, without intrusive commentary, to a work of art with its own integrity, which in some way raises the same issues as the passion story, or echoes its narrative or symbolic structure. We want them to experience some of the same range of emotions and aesthetic responses, without their being labeled as "stock" responses to a canonized sacred story.

This is not an easy set of standards to meet in forty-five minutes. Unfortunately, religious films that don't go in for heavy literalism tend to go in for heavy allegory, or real-life drama aimed at an audience from junior high upwards. But there are a few films that can give what we are looking for, and that are generally available for rent from Christian education resource centers or film catalogs. Good stories, some of them available as sound recordings and others only for reading aloud or telling, and traditional folk tales, fairy tales, and classics of children's literature are frequently much better choices than avowedly "religious" material.

You should always preview any film or recording that you are thinking of using with the children, and any equipment that will be needed to show or play it should be set up in advance and checked to be sure that it's in good working order and that you know how to run it. Nothing is more destructive of the mood and flow of a day like Palm Saturday than to spend twenty minutes sweating over a film projector.

And perhaps most important of all (and most surprising to your usual thinking as a teacher): *do not discuss the movie, recording, or story.* Let them think of it as an interlude, even as a bit of secular relief in the middle of a heavily ecclesiastical day. If you have chosen a story that is rich and suggestive, the last thing you want to do with it is imply that it's a lesson with a moral to decode. You want them to get the idea, deep down inside where they don't even examine it, that there is a pattern in *life*, not just in Sunday school or church but *in the world, where the rest of their lives are lived*, and that this pattern is one of life out of death, joy out of suffering, renewal out of sacrificial love. And you want them to make this discovery themselves.

(5) *Worship* (no more than thirty minutes) - Worship is, of course, implicit in everything we do all day and may become explicit as part of the storytelling format if something like the Prayer Walk described in the following chapter is used. When the afternoon activity is coming to an end, we clean up, and gather in the room that has been our base of operations all day. The children show each other their work, relax and unwind a little, and share a snack—usually pretzels or tiny loaves made from the bread dough that also went into bread sculpture and eucharistic loaves. Every-

one is always very thirsty, and a snack of fresh bread, though delicious and eagerly eaten, adds to their thirst, so be sure you have plenty of juice and perhaps some apples or grapes as well. Parents begin to drift in. It's time to gather in prayer and take leave of each other.

We have sometimes ended with a eucharist. It is usually not a good idea, however: children are tired, and surfeited with religious imagery. But if it's important to you that a eucharist should be part of what you do, you should make sure the priest is there for enough of the day to be able to make it a genuine offering. It's particularly important that the worship continue the emphasis on depth and transcendence that you have been building into the whole day. Priests who are not used to working with children may assume that children's worship should always follow an academic model: they may treat the worship as a kind of instructed eucharist, interrupting sacramental actions with a lot of explanations; or they may insist on quizzing children about what they have done and learned. This honest mistake can go far toward breaking down what you have worked so hard to build.

It's often more feasible to point out, perfectly truthfully, that the eucharist that wraps up Palm Saturday is the parish eucharist on Palm Sunday, and you expect to see everyone there. Arranging now to have children carry banners they have made, reminding them that their bread will be offered on the altar—these can make specific connections and even elicit a commitment to be there. If you know the special characteristics of the parish Holy Week celebrations, you can build into Palm Saturday some explicit anticipations of them, thus achieving from the opposite direction, in a sense, the function of the eucharist as gathering and offering of what you have done this day.

The day itself can end simply by gathering the children into a circle, and holding hands. Have the kids shut their eyes and take several deep breaths, slower and slower. Speak to them in a slow, peaceful voice. Remind them that God has been with them all day as they have listened, worked, learned, and shared. Now God is still with them, in each of them and in all of them together: God is in his church, and the church is us. Tomorrow we will begin to re-live, together in the church, the terrible and wonderful things that Jesus did to bring us back to God. We do not understand this story with our minds, but with our hearts; and we are deeply thankful for what Jesus did for us. We want to love him, and be close to him; we want to share the new life he has won for us, and let him make us new in love and peace.

A simple prayer, to which the children say "Amen," can follow. Or an even simpler prayer, such as "Thank you, Jesus," can be said, perhaps several times over, by all of you together.

We like to end with singing: in this case, something simple, re-petitive, and meditative. If your parish uses music from Taizé and the children know it, it would be perfect here; otherwise, "Long Live God" from *Godspell* is our perennial favorite. Break the spell with the peace, and watch them go. You will be left with a full heart, an unspeakably weary body, and (even if the kids have done a lot of clean-up) an appallingly messy Sunday school space. Never mind. It's worth it.

# Chapter 14

# Something Strange is Happening

The Prayer Walk of the Passion that highlights our Palm Saturday celebration is, in some ways, a variation on the Stations of the Cross, a devotional pattern through which the church (intuitively balancing instruction, storytelling, meditation, movement, and liturgy) has told its central story for many generations. The stations, however, focus very narrowly on one chapter of the passion, passing over the events preceding Jesus' trial, and stopping short of the resurrection. While this focus and the spirituality it reflects have a real integrity and validity, that was not the story we wished to tell. Like the stations of the cross, however, the Prayer Walk treads the very fine line between story, prayer, liturgy, and play. It draws for some of its symbolic vocabulary on our own parish's Holy Week customs (footwashing at the Maundy Thursday liturgy, Tenebrae on Good Friday); it also hints at the vocabulary of the Great Vigil in its enactment of the descent into hell.

The Prayer Walk was designed to echo and amplify an activity that we had done in the same space and time slot for the previous All Saints' Day. (See the next chapter, "The Communion of Saints.") Both proved to be so effective that we now repeat them annually. The All Saints' activity (a "Halloween funhouse") opens in pitch darkness in a tower stairwell, where we tell the creation story and strike a light. We then move by candlelight through the narthex and up the center aisle to the altar, playing on the way with the stories of Adam and Eve, Noah, Jonah, the Exodus, the coming of Jesus, and his death and resurrection. Approaching the font and the altar, the children renounce Satan, receive Christ's seal on their foreheads, and eat a morsel of angel cake with a sip of grape juice. Then, coming at last into the brightly lit chancel, they are welcomed by the communion of saints.

In the Palm Saturday Prayer Walk, we work in the opposite direction: we move from Lady Chapel to altar, down the center aisle, then out into narthex, pitch-dark stairwell, and finally down the stairs and out the doors into the spring sunshine (or the spring rain) in the small garden beside the church. The tower stairwell, easily the most exciting part of the journey both times, functions once as the the womb of creation and once as the tomb of Christ—the womb of the new creation.

(a) *The Triumphal Entry.* Each group of twelve children troops into the chapel, carrying bunches of palms in their hands. A bearded man, dressed in an alb (with the hood up), takes the part of Jesus, and is waiting out of sight, by the chapel door, as I gather the children round. "Let's pretend," I say to them. "This is long, long ago, in Jerusalem—we're here to celebrate the Passover, the festival of our freedom from slavery in Egypt. But we're not free. The Romans are ruling our country! Are we happy about that?" "No!" they chorus. "What do we want?" I holler. "Freedom!" they reply (with a little prompting from me). "When do we want it?" "NOW!!"[1]

"Listen!" I tell them in a quieter, but excited voice. "I've heard that God is about to act to set us free! I've heard that the Messiah has come to earth—that the famous preacher, Jesus of Nazareth, is the Messiah! They say he's coming today, to Jerusalem, to celebrate the Passover. Do you think he's coming? Do you think he'll fight the Romans? Do you think we'll see him?"

One child is sent to the door to look, and encounters "Jesus" coming in. I launch the children (who are really getting into the swing of it by now) into cries of "Hosanna! The Messiah!" and have them wave their palms and follow "Jesus" as he passes silently through the chapel to stand by the altar in the darkened church. "Come on! Let's follow him! Let's see where he goes! Let's be his disciples!"

(b) *The Last Supper.* There are chairs set for the children in a semicircle behind the free-standing altar. On the altar are six lighted candles (here and elsewhere, the candles used are of the hurricane type, in tall glass jars), a plate of matzoh, a stemmed glass full of grape juice, and a supply of paper napkins. On the floor we have placed a pitcher of warm water, a basin, and a supply of thick towels.

I tell them, very briefly, of the Last Supper, how Jesus celebrated the Passover with his friends and gave a new and mysterious meaning to its symbols of bread and wine. "Jesus" stands at the altar, facing the children. Silently, he lifts and breaks the matzoh, and distributes it and the cup to the children. As they eat, I tell how Jesus warned them that one of them would betray him, and how, in their eagerness to show their loyalty, the disciples began to quarrel and brag about which of them would be most important and special when Jesus became the king, and how Jesus did something to help them understand how they must live if they were to be his friends.

Then we have the children remove their shoes and socks, and "Jesus" kneels down and washes their feet. Children who are reluctant to comply are not forced; most are very willing. We talk quietly about how it feels to have your feet washed, and who is likely to do such a thing for you. The principal of your school? The president of the United States? Your mother? A nurse if you are sick and in the hospital? The most important doctor in the hospital? Your father? The priest in our church? Your best friend? When all the feet are washed, "Jesus" goes back into the chapel.

(c) *The Arrest, Trial, and Crucifixion.*[2] As the children finish putting on their shoes, I begin to tell how Jesus left the supper with his disciples...went into a garden to pray...he was lonely and sad, and frightened of what God was asking him to do...he begged his friends to keep him company, but they all fell asleep...one of his friends had taken sides with his enemies, and showed them where to find him...Judas came up to Jesus, and kissed him...the soldiers and guardsmen arrested him and hustled him away...his friends all ran away and hid.

*A child is asked to blow out the first candle.*

Jesus was taken to the High Priest's house...the High Priests were enemies of Jesus because they were scared that Jesus might take away their power...they had collected witnesses to tell lies about him...all the powerful religious leaders agreed that Jesus should be killed...Peter had crept into the High Priest's house and was sitting warming his hands by the fire, when a doorkeeper recognized him as Jesus' friend...Peter panicked and pretended he had never even heard of Jesus—Peter, who had bragged about how brave he would be...Jesus, being led out to Pilate, looked at Peter...Peter cried bitterly.

*A child is asked to blow out the second candle.*

Jesus was taken to Pilate, the Roman governor, because only the Roman government could order someone to be killed...the Romans used to set one prisoner free every Passover, to keep the people quiet...a crowd had gathered, ready to call for the release of Barabbas, a famous terrorist...*(here I cheerlead one side of the arc of children in calling for Barabbas)*...Pilate thought the trial of Jesus was not a fair one, and tried to let Jesus go, but the crowd was determined to have Barabbas *("Barabbas! Barabbas!")*...when Pilate brought out Jesus instead, some of them began to yell for Jesus *(cheerleading again, this time for "Jesus! Jesus!")* but most of them thought he was trying to trick them, and they yelled, "CRUCIFY HIM! CRUCIFY HIM!" till Pilate was scared there would be a fight in the street...*(more cheerleading, then I let it die down)* so he sent for a bowl of water, *(I wash my hands, using the water bowl that*

*"Jesus" used when he washed their feet)*, and he washed his hands, to show it was not his idea and not his fault.

*A child is asked to blow out the third candle.*

The soldiers took Jesus off and made fun of him...they made him dress up like a king and wear a crown of sharp thorns...they pretended to bow down to him...then they whipped him and punched him and spat at him...he was made to carry his cross to a hill called Golgotha.

*A child blows out the fourth candle.*

Jesus was nailed to the cross...his mother and two of his friends were there watching, staying with him, not caring if it got them into trouble...nearly everybody who saw what was happening started to laugh at Jesus and make fun of him because it looked as if he couldn't be the Messiah after all.

*A child blows out the fifth candle.*

Even though it was the middle of the day, the sky grew dark...Jesus called out, "MY GOD, MY GOD, WHY HAVE YOU ABANDONED ME??!"...he bowed his head and died...As the sun was setting, his friends took his body and buried it in a cave that had been cut from a hillside, and they rolled a great stone over the door.

*A child blows out the sixth and last candle.*
*Silence.*

(d) *Procession of the Cross.* We sing verse one of Hymn 172, "Were you there when they crucified my Lord?" Then I take the processional cross, heft it to lie lengthwise along the shoulders of as many of the kids as possible, and help them carry it slowly down the center aisle, singing verse two, "Were you there when they nailed him to the tree?" They approach the doorway of the tower staircase, where the cross is leaned against the wall as we sing the final verse, "Were you there when they laid him in the tomb?" and the children enter the dark stairwell one by one. They have to crouch down or even crawl in order to do this, because the entrance has been partially blocked by a very large sheet of corrugated cardboard with a very small doorway cut into it, and painted to represent the tomb of Jesus.

(e) *Descent into Hell, and Resurrection*. All the children creep into the stairwell and grope their way down the stairs, which in April are ice-cold as well as pitch dark. I describe to them how Jesus' body was buried in a cold, dark tomb. Jesus was dead—he had gone to the place where the dead were. I ask them to pretend that we too are dead. I point out to them that in Jesus' time the people of Israel did not expect that when they died they would "go to heaven"; rather, they expected to wait in silence and darkness until the time when God would come to them, set them free, and raise them to new life. When all the children are clustered at the foot of the stairs, straining their eyes in the dark, I begin to play a tape, on which is recorded this adaptation of a Holy Saturday sermon of Saint Euthemius the Great:

> Something strange is happening—there is a great silence on earth today. The whole earth is silent, because the King of heaven and earth is dead. God has died, and hell trembles with fear.
>
> Jesus has gone to the place of the dead, to search for Adam and Eve and for all who have gone down to darkness and the shadow of death. Jesus approaches them, bearing the Cross, the weapon that has won him the victory. He takes them by the hand, and raises them up, and this is what he says:
>
> "Awake, sleepers, and rise from the dead, and Christ will give you light! Rise from the dead, for I am the life of the dead. Out of love for you, I, your God, became a human being, and came to earth. For your sake, I died today upon earth. You once reached out to take fruit from a tree, and to save you, I have been nailed to a tree. You were driven out of Paradise, and I have come to lead you to heaven. I did not create you to be held prisoner for ever.
>
> "Rise up! let us leave this place—for I have died with you, and you shall rise with me. The Kingdom of Heaven has been prepared for you from all eternity."[3]

As the voice cries out, "Awake, sleepers!" the first soft sustained note of the finale of *Godspell* begins to be heard on the tape, growing louder as the speech of Christ continues. At that moment, a faint, warm light begins to illumine the rough plaster walls of the stairwell, and then, round the curve of the stairs, "Jesus" comes among us, carrying a single candle. Wordlessly, he passes among the awestruck children, then, reaching the exit doorway at the bottom of the stairs, he turns to face them. As the tape ends, with the crescendo of "Long live God...Prepare ye the way of the Lord!" he flings open the door, and leads them through the small downstairs lobby (past the flabbergasted ballet students and parents who are gathered there for Saturday classes at the ballet school that rents our undercroft space) and out into the fresh spring air. They are laughing and jumping up and down with the release of suspense.

If the weather is good, we shove trowels and flats of pansies into their hands and leave them in the care of a teenager, while we take the next group of twelve through the Prayer Walk. If it is raining (as it has been for the majority of the Palm Saturdays since we started the Prayer Walk), we run along the sidewalk to the door of the parish hall, shouting, "We're alive! We're alive!" and I make sure to sing with them, at some point during the day, the song that includes the verse

> The fields were green as green could be
> When from his glorious seat
> Our Lord, our God he watered us
> With his heavenly dew so sweet.[4]

The children are spellbound by this experience. There is hardly ever any inattention, embarrassment, resistance, or silliness. (It helps that some of the littlest children have their parents along.) I have even had, to my astonishment, more than one child request to repeat the Prayer Walk a second time in the same morning.

Crucial to its effectiveness, I think, are three elements: a theology of *Christus Victor*, focusing on Christ's victory over the powers of death and hell; a sensory or "hands-on" approach, involving the whole child, at every stage in the journey; and an aura of mystery, especially surrounding the figure of Jesus. The actor playing Jesus never speaks, and his face is shadowed by the hood of his alb: the children are free, to some extent, to invest this figure with their own imaginative material according to their own spirituality and inner need.

These are the elements that make good liturgy for adults, and I am increasingly convinced that children's liturgical needs are not qualitatively different from those of adults. Good liturgy makes images, and for children the images need to be drawn with a broader brush, in brighter colors. Sensory as well as verbal experiences are crucial; doing must go along with listening and watching. But children do not require a separate symbolic vocabulary, limited to terms with which they are already entirely familiar through their daily lives. Nor do they need a different liturgical grammar, in which symbols are always being reduced to mere signs with a single predetermined meaning, or in which worship is made lighthearted or "fun" or relieved of all distressing or ambiguous content. Children do not need to have our story translated from poetry into prose for their benefit. They need, just as we do, to be invited to fall in love, and dance before the Lord.

# NOTES

1. Kyle McGee, rector of St. Paul's 1987-1991, taught me to use these echoes of the Civil Rights movement, which are great ice breakers as well as good theology.

2. Some of the connecting narrative links in the story as outlined here derive from Dorothy Sayer's superb series of radio plays on the life of Christ, *The Man Born to be King* (Harper & Row, 1943). A careful reading of the four Passion plays in the cycle is an excellent way to prepare for an extemporaneous telling of the story to children.

3. Adapted from *A Triduum Sourcebook*, ed. Gabe Huck and Mary Ann Simcoe (Archdiocese of Chicago: Liturgy Training Publications, 1983), p. 64.

4. "The Bellman's Song," *Oxford Book of Carols*, no. 46.

## Chapter 15

# The Communion of Saints

ALL SAINTS' DAY BLENDS marvelously with the part of the year in which it falls—the season of very late Pentecost, a kind of pre-Advent culminating in the feast of Christ the King. The Scriptures in this season speak of the return of the Son of Man; the last days; the vindication of God's holy people out of struggle, loss, and pain; the fulfillment of the kingdom. As the wind strips the leaves from the trees and living things retreat before the advancing cold and darkness, the church gathers to reaffirm our most ancient hope: that God has called us, as a people, into eternal life—life that transcends time, loss, and decay, and overcomes the Evil One, the destroyer, the spiritual forces of wickedness that rebel against God, the powers of darkness that tempt and corrupt and terrorize and go bump in the night.

The Prayer Book encourages us, therefore, to celebrate Holy Baptism at All Saints', welcoming new members into the communion of saints and affording us all the opportunity to reaffirm our faith through the renunciation of Satan, the affirmation of the baptismal creed, and the renewal of baptismal vows. *We believe in the*

*holy catholic Church, the communion of saints, the forgiveness of sins,*
*the resurrection of the body, and the life everlasting.*

Most church school curriculums give little space to All Saints'
Day, or indeed to any of the matters raised in the last paragraph of
the baptismal creed, or to baptism itself. The deep and fertile connections that can be drawn between All Saints' Day, baptism, and
Halloween are not immediately obvious; we need to think long
and hard about what story we actually want to tell on this day.
Probably the first thing that many parishes try in an effort to celebrate All Saints' with children, cross-fertilized by Halloween, is a
simple costume party in which children dress up as saints. That
sounds like a good idea, but it runs the risk of sabotage by children who will not readily give up the spooks and the devils. And
they are right.

Any attempt to celebrate All Saints' Day with children that
looks only to the parading of saints and heroes is presenting only
one side of the story: the winners. Why celebrate the winners without doing justice to their struggle? Children know that life is a
struggle. We need to show them that we are not afraid to name
our adversaries as well as our heroes, that we even dare to *dress up*
as our adversary and pretend to *be* the enemy—for then, when we
take off the costume, we are proving that we can resist the enemy
and reclaim our selfhood. We need to acknowledge how hard the
struggle is and how even the bravest suffer fears and setbacks and
temptations to join the other side, and how they have won their
victory only by the gracious help of God and the loving help of
their brothers and sisters, and (like their Lord) only by death. In so
doing we do not frighten children, we reassure them, for now they
know we are telling the truth.

There are Christian bodies and Christian families that will not
allow their children to participate in Halloween at all, because of
its ancient connections with paganism and its continuing association with devils, witches, and monsters. These Christians are
frightened of letting their children participate in such traditions, in
the same way some other parents are afraid of letting their children
play with toy guns. They fear that permitting children to play with

a symbol of evil—the gun or the devil mask—signals to them that we approve of the evil itself, and removes all restraints on its seductive powers.

But by censoring children's imaginative lives, by modeling fear and denial instead of an imaginative approach to our own destructive impulses, we fail to help our children. We are warning them that we ourselves are so frightened of our own aggression that we cannot face it or offer hope that it can be tamed. This realization may be more frightening to children than the fear they certainly feel as they themselves play with and test these symbols of evil, and find their own response. Censorship may also, of course, have the opposite effect of endowing these ideas and figures with the fascination of forbidden fruit.

By the same token, we miss the point of All Saints' Day if our message consists only of, "The saints of God are just folk like me, and I mean to be one too." It may be important to bring the idea of holiness down from the stained glass and into the real world, but children will do that all by themselves if we tell them stories they can really own. Their most serious, formative, permanent work of learning and growth occurs in their imaginative worlds— worlds of heroic adventure, scary monsters, and lovely princesses. The message, "We're all special—we're all saints," is a truism that contains the seeds of its own negation. If everyone is a saint, then what is so special about being one? The word *saint* becomes merely a pious synonym for *person*, or perhaps *nice person*, and we have reduced the glorious promise of the gospel to yet another grown-up, therapeutic affirmation that everybody is special and unique and wonderful.

One does not convince children they are wonderful simply by telling them so. Instead, we need to speak their language by telling them stories in which someone small and despised and rejected goes forth into a very big and scary world, confronts evil and triumphs over it (even at great risk, perhaps even at great cost), and emerges vindicated and with blessings to share with the community. Unless we impart the image of a saint as someone *transfigured through struggle, sacrifice, and faith by a glory from beyond the world,* why should it excite children to sing, "And I mean to be one too"?

All Saints' Day is about the baptismal mystery: we are all saints because in our baptism we have put on Christ and asked him to conform us to his life of love, struggle, sacrifice, and vindication, which is the pattern for our lives and the life of the people of God in history and in community. The story we want to tell and keep on telling is the record of God's saving deeds in history. On All Saints' Saturday we are trying to invite the children into an encounter with the baptismal themes of God acting through water and the Spirit; with the image of a chosen people, washed and anointed and fed and sent into the world; with death and resurrection, fear and hope. And, not least, we are encouraging them to confront the figure of Satan—his terrifying power, his seductive attractiveness—and to claim as their own our conviction that in choosing Christ and renouncing Satan we can be free of that seductiveness and power. We accept the Halloween spooks into All Saints' Day, because we particularly want to remind ourselves that by the might of Christ we can exorcise them.

The schedule for All Saints' Saturday is our classic pattern, based on a vivid, dramatic storytelling experience in the church itself, several craft projects, lunch (brought from home), a movie or video, and (brief) closing worship. Our favorite craft activities for All Saints' Saturday, as for many of our Saturdays, include banner making and bread baking. Banner making can provide a device for assigning "family homework" in advance of All Saints' Day: we ask families to choose a saint (who must be someone who has died) and learn something about his or her life so that the children will have ideas for their banners on Saturday. We try to include bread baking in every Saturday we celebrate, as an unspoken lesson on the importance of bread in our common life. The bread we make is used in the next morning's eucharist; some of it also becomes our afternoon snack together, and lately we have learned to create spectacular bread sculptures for the whole parish to enjoy at coffee hour. All Saints' Day motifs for the bread sculpture have included St. George and the dragon, Jonah and the whale, and the tree of life.

In some years we have visited a local cemetery to make rubbings of seventeenth-century gravestones with newsprint and crayons. To touch on resurrection as well as death, another group planted hundreds of bulbs on the edge of the church lawn. Other activities that change from year to year depending on the available talents in the congregation have included mask making, story and poetry writing (using the lectionary readings for All Saints', especially the reading from Revelation 7), and yarn dyeing using natural materials. There is always a book table, with stories of the lives of Christian heroes and stories about death and dying. When there is a baptism the next day, we decorate baptismal candles for the candidates.

The high point of All Saints' Saturday is its opening activity, our "Halloween funhouse." We have a huge old Victorian building, and part of the fun is to use the building creatively so that we are teaching *about* the church at the same time as we are having fun *in* the church. Anyone else trying to adapt this idea would need to work with the architecture and layout of their own building—and also take the number of children into account. We find we can lead no more than twelve children at a time through the funhouse; that usually means three groups all told, which takes a little over an hour.

(1) *Creation.* We begin in a circular stairwell that runs up inside one of our towers, opening into the narthex at the rear of the nave. A teenager ushers the children in from the basement, and they come up one flight in total darkness. By the time they reach the place where I am waiting for them they are always thoroughly and delightedly spooked. I talk to them about the darkness and emptiness that preceded God's work of creation. I have a homemade sound-effects tape, and I turn it on to play the first two verses of Genesis 1, with a background of the *Ode to Joy* from Beethoven's Ninth Symphony. As the tape says "Let there be light!" and the music swells, I light a candle, revealing that the stairwell is lined with six banners, representing the six days of creation, that the

Sunday school children made for the first production of our Easter pageant. As they admire the banners, I talk about the beautiful place that God made for his people to live in. All they had to do was obey him and care for his world. I open the door to the narthex, saying, "Let's come into the beautiful place God has made for us—let's see what happens to God's people there."

(2) *The Fall.* (Episodes 2 through 6 take place in our large narthex, in very dim light.) Right outside the tower door stands a potted tree, hung with gumdrops. On the floor around it are about two dozen stuffed animals. As the children gather round, I tell them that they can look at the tree, play with the animals, or do anything else they like—except take the candy. A kind-looking adult emerges from behind the door, and at that moment I suddenly pretend to have forgotten something important and to have to run out for a minute. I tell the children, "I'll be right back—in the meantime, Kelly (indicating the new adult) will take care of you," and I duck out. The minute I'm out of sight, Kelly sets to work convincing the children that I couldn't have meant what I said, the candy is obviously meant to be eaten, if they take just one each nobody will ever notice, and so on. Most of them cooperate quite readily, though the older kids and the seasoned veterans know perfectly well what it is all about and enjoy baiting the tempter and stringing out this episode as long as they can. When nearly all of them have capitulated and are munching their gumdrops, I come back in. "Oh, no!" I cry. "What have you done?"—and Kelly, who had slipped away when I returned, now reappears with a horrible laugh, extravagantly costumed in devil horns and cape, and carrying a red pitchfork. "Ha ha! Now I've caught you!" says Satan. "You've broken God's law. You're lost forever! God will throw you out and forsake you!"

(3) *The Flood.* Next to the tree is a rocking boat from the church nursery. "God's people had to leave the beautiful place where God had meant for them to live," I tell the children. "And as they lived in the world, they became more and more wicked and evil. Finally, God decided to wipe them all out and start over—all except a special few, and the animals...." I invite them to load the animals

into the boat, and climb in themselves, while the tape plays vivid wind-and-water sounds (easy to create in any bathroom, by turning on the shower and sloshing water vigorously in the tub, while blowing into the microphone). As the kids rock back and forth in the little boat, Satan pokes them with his pitchfork, gleefully predicting that the rain will never end, they will all drown, God doesn't care what happens to them—but the water noises on the tape do end, and everybody climbs back out of the boat.

(4) *Jonah and the Whale.* (This scene is out of historical order, so that we can end this section with the Exodus.) Two paper eyes fastened to a vinyl "play tunnel" make a convincing whale—actually it looks more like a lamprey, but nobody seems to mind. The tape plays a portion of Debussy's *La Mer* and selections from Jonah's prayer from the belly of the whale, though it's hard to hear over the noises the kids make, getting inside and then being vomited out (or, quite unscripturally, emerging at the back end of the whale).

(5) *Slavery in Egypt.* A big bucket stands by the door, along with a pile of bricks. After the briefest introduction ("Once upon a time, God's people were slaves in Egypt, and their rulers made them work and work and work"), both Satan and I start to yell at the kids to "load the bricks in the bucket! Now carry them over there! Build a tower with them! Faster! What's the matter with you, are you lazy? That's no good! Take it down! Put the bricks back in the bucket! Come on, get moving!!!" They do as they are told, with some anxiety and confusion; it usually takes several minutes before they complain or rebel. When they do, I say, "And God heard the cry of the children of Israel, and set them free ...."

(6) *The Exodus.* The double glass doors into the nave have been draped with plastic dropcloths to suggest "walls of water to the right of them and to the left of them." The teenage guide and I swing them open and the kids pass through in triumph, with Beethoven's Ninth going full blast—and Satan left behind.

(7) *The Gift of God's Son.* (The next section takes place in the dimly lit rear of the nave.) I gather the children round, and have them sit on the floor and calm down after the excitement of their

adventures so far. I tell them that even in the promised land God's people continued to be disobedient. "So God did a new thing—" and I have them close their eyes, and hand around a tiny cuddly baby doll wrapped in a cloth, asking them to feel it, guess what it is, but not tell. This is a marvelously calming device, and creates a whole new mood, of awe and wonder. Then they open their eyes and we talk about God's gift to us of Jesus, who came as a tiny baby and lived and grew with us.

(8) *Jesus' Death and New Life.* I speak briefly about Jesus' ministry, and how his enemies arrested him and killed him on a cross. I bring out from behind the last pew a banner the children made some years ago, showing Jesus on the cross. Telling of Jesus' burial, I roll up the banner and lay it under the pew, then bring out from the same place another banner, showing the risen Lord. We clap and cheer, and jump up from the floor, ready to follow Jesus in our own lives.

(9) *The Church and our Part in It.* Now begins a slow journey up the center aisle, stopping several times. The first stop is the font, which has been placed partway up the center aisle, with the paschal candle burning next to it. Here we decide we want to belong to Jesus. We turn back toward the door into the narthex, where we can see the figure of Satan, silhouetted on the other side of the glass door. As loud as we can, we shout, "I RENOUNCE YOU, SATAN!" and are rewarded by a howl of agony and the sound of Satan falling to the floor. More claps and cheers. Then we wet the children's heads, stamp their foreheads with a cross (carved from a cut potato and inked on a red stamp pad; the first time we did this, we didn't realize the ink was permanent).

The next stop is the food basket, in which we collect canned goods on Sunday mornings. Because followers of Jesus share his work of doing good, we put in token cans of food from a stack that is set nearby. The last stop is the altar, spread with a white cloth and set with lighted candles. Here the children receive a morsel of angel food cake and a sip of grape juice, and we talk about how God feeds us as we journey together through life.

Dividing the altar from the chancel area is a very large movable bulletin board, with flannel on both sides—on the near side, facing the children, the flannel is dark navy blue, almost black, and bears a design in cut-out felt that is clearly a Halloween motif: a graveyard full of crosses under a huge full moon, with a twisted leafless tree, its last orange leaves flying off from it in the wind. There are more felt crosses in a little pile on the altar—enough for all of us. This is what awaits us at the end of our journey; we acknowledge this explicitly by having each child take a cross and add it to the scene. Then, having done this, they pass to the other side of the bulletin board, into the brilliantly lit chancel, to the accompaniment once more of the *Ode to Joy.*

(11) *The Church Triumphant.* The reverse of the bulletin board is backed in brilliant royal blue and has a design of the Lamb of God, surrounded by abstract flame-like shapes in red, orange, yellow, and green, and by many simple felt figures in white robes, their arms uplifted in praise. As with the crosses, there are enough additional figures so that each child may add one to the communion of saints. The newcomers are loudly and enthusiastically welcomed to the kingdom by a teacher and (the later groups) by the other kids who have preceded them through the funhouse. They are no longer dead, they are saints, alive forever in the presence of the Lamb who was slain. The teacher invites them to join whatever is going on here in the chancel, which varies from year to year— sometimes they make banners representing their chosen saints, sometimes they make crowns and robes for themselves, or shields with symbols on them for their own faith and gifts as saints.

Whatever is made here in the kingdom is brought into church the next day in the All Saints' procession. Inevitably, the last group to join the kingdom has far less time to work on this project than the first, but this does not seem to bother them as much as we would have expected. Logistically, a communal project such as a mural or a few large banners would make more sense, but the children have a strong and sound liturgical instinct that tells them it is vital that they each have their own emblem to carry in the procession that celebrates the sainthood of all the baptized.

Year after year, the children are entranced by this whole experience. It enters their communal memory and is looked forward to, remembered, and tantalizingly described to younger classmates and newcomers. Two anecdotes stand out in my own recollection from the first time we did it. The first is a conversation with David, the eighth grader who so devotedly shepherded three groups of children through the funhouse. As we were cleaning up, he said, "Gretchen, I have a suggestion." I steeled myself for constructive criticism, and David went on, "I really think we should do this again next year—because the *kids* enjoyed it so much." Which, as we all know, is the eighth grader's way of saying, "Because *I* enjoyed it so much."

The second is from the next day's baptismal liturgy. The sponsors and parents seemed hesitant and confused as they made the baptismal promises, and the words, "Do you renounce Satan and all the spiritual forces of wickedness that rebel against God?" were answered by a barely audible "I renounce them." Clustered round the font, with the red ink still faintly visible on their foreheads, several children turned baffled faces to me and whispered, "Why don't they say that *louder?*"

# Chapter 16

# A Corpus Christi
# Celebration

HE LITURGY OF THE Feast of Corpus Christi, developed in the thirteenth century by Thomas Aquinas, provided the medieval church with an opportunity to focus on Christ's gift of the eucharist in a context outside of Holy Week, and therefore to give it a more festal character. Corpus Christi, celebrated on the Thursday following Trinity Sunday, became a major early-summer festival, with fairs, mystery plays, and a general holiday atmosphere. A revival of this feast for the children of our parish has given us the focus for an end-of-year celebration, and an opportunity to explore the mystery of the eucharist in rich and suggestive ways.

Our children do not receive formal first communion preparation, because they are fed at the Lord's table from the day of their baptism. We therefore need to develop a different structure from the "first communion class" for bringing the children together around the theme of the eucharist. Corpus Christi Saturday, as we call it, has proved to be a well-loved annual event for the whole Sunday school, drawing in many eucharistic themes, heightening the children's awareness of the sacrament and its centrality to our life together, and helping them feel more at home with our forms of worship.

Corpus Christi Saturday is celebrated in early June, just after Pentecost. Unlike our other Saturdays, which run from morning to early afternoon, Corpus Christi begins at 3:00 p.m. and ends at 7:00 with supper for the children, their parents, the clergy, and the teachers. The structure of the day is taken from the structure of the eucharistic liturgy: *coming together, listening and learning, praying and sharing, breaking bread, and going out.*[1]

As with some of our other Saturdays, we assign "homework" in advance. Families are asked to choose a food that holds special meaning for them, and have their children help them to prepare it for the potluck supper that ends the day. They are also asked to talk with their children about celebrations that are special in their families.

There has been little variation in the structure and content of the day since our first celebration in the spring of 1987. We began that day with *coming together*, a half hour or so of preparation for the afternoon's activities. As the children arrived, they were shown into our Lady Chapel, where we sang "Let Us Break Bread Together on our Knees" (Hymn 325 in the 1982 Hymnal), and I explained to them the program for the rest of the day. Then I read them *The Tale of John Barleycorn*, an old English folk song.[2] Before actually reading the book, we talked together about food: how all our food comes from living things that are harvested or cut down or even killed so that we may live and grow and be strong and healthy. I explained how, long ago, people thought of the life of their crops as if it were a human life, or the life of a god: when the seed was planted, they thought of a dead person being buried; when it grew, it was like a miracle—a dead person coming back to life. Then, just when it has grown tall and beautiful, the grain is cut and threshed and ground: it is as if the grain has suffered and died, giving up its life for us.

"Beer was an important food to English people long ago," I said. "It was almost like bread and wine all rolled together. It was made of grain and yeast, like bread; it was a drink that made you cheerful or even drunk, like wine. Drinking beer with your friends was a way to celebrate the good things in your life. And whenever you drank the beer, you would remember where it came from—how it was made from grain that was buried and grew and was cut down and ground up; how the seed gave its life so we could have this beer to drink—and you would be glad and thankful."

The book, *The Tale of John Barleycorn*, is illustrated with beautiful, vigorous woodcuts. In many of the cuts, a small face is visible within the sheaf of barley: the face of "John Barleycorn," the personified grain. I read the verses, and we sang the song a couple of times.³ Then I ushered the children into the next hour's activities.

This hour was devoted to *listening and learning*. The church itself had been turned into a "Corpus Christi Fair," with five "booths" based on five ways of looking at the eucharist. The five themes we had chosen were: *celebration, sharing our faith with others (who may be different from us), giving thanks (offering sacrifice), telling a story,* and *a meal around a table*. Each booth was located in a place within the church that connected in some way to the theme being developed in that booth, since we wanted the children to learn about the use of our worship space by actually using it in ways that relate, subliminally, to how it is used on Sunday morning. Children were asked to choose a booth to start with; after that they were free to roam.

The *celebration* booth was set up at the rear of the church, by the main doors. Several adults were there with cupcakes and party hats, fancy paper plates and napkins, and a bulletin board covered with brightly colored paper. One adult had an instant camera, and took pictures of the children in their party hats. The children were asked to describe a celebration in their own families. Their remarks were written down on construction paper and put up on the bulletin board along with their pictures.

*Giving thanks and offering sacrifice* was our John Barleycorn booth. It was held on the open space out in front of the altar. A fiddler had joined us, and each group of children visiting the booth mimed and danced the burial, rebirth, life, and passion of the grain.

One child was chosen as John Barleycorn, and given a green satin jester's collar with bells, and two stalks of the lovely tall marsh grass that grows everywhere on the Connecticut shoreline. One was a dried, feathery stalk of last year's grass that had stood all winter, and one a bright green spear of the new spring growth that at this time of year is rapidly shooting up from the roots of the brown stalks. The fiddler fiddled and the children sang, circling in a ring (once around, then back the other way) on the refrain:

There were three men come from the west
Their fortunes for to try;
And these three men made a solemn vow
John Barleycorn must die:
John Barleycorn must die.
They buried him three furrows deep          *"John Barleycorn" lies on*
Laid clods upon his head;                         *the floor and is covered*
And these three men made a solemn vow    *with a length of brown felt.*
John Barleycorn was dead:                        *The other children wag*
John Barleycorn was dead.                         *their fingers gloatingly*

Fa la la la, it's a lovely day...                      *The children circle in a ring*

They let him lie for a very long time          *The children pantomime the*
Till the rain from heaven did fall;              *falling rain*
Then little Sir John sprang up his head       *"John Barleycorn" pokes up*
And he so amazed them all:                         *the green shoot, then stands*
He so amazed them all.                                *up*

They let him stand till the Midsummer Day
When he looked both pale and wan;
Then little Sir John he grew a long beard      *"John Barleycorn" exchanges*
And he so became a man:                              *the green shoot for the*
He so became a man.                                     *dry one*

Fa la la la...                                                   *Circle in a ring again*

| | |
|---|---|
| They have hired men with the scythe so sharp | *The children swing imaginary scythes, and "John Barleycorn"* |
| To cut him off at the knee; | *and the grass stalk drop in a heap* |
| They have rolled him and tied him around the waist, | |
| They served him barbarously... | *The children mime the rolling and tying...* |
| | |
| They have hired men with the crab-tree sticks | |
| To cut him skin from bone; | *...and fierce blows* |
| And the miller he has served him worse than that, | *...and grinding* |
| He's ground him between two stones... | |
| | |
| Fa la la la... | *Circle in a ring again* |
| | |
| They have wheeled him here, they have wheeled him there, | *Mime the wheeling in a barrow* |
| They've wheeled him to a barn, | |
| And the brewer he has served him worse than that, | *...and plunging in a vat* |
| He's bunged him in a vat... | |
| | |
| They have worked their will on John Barleycorn | *"John Barleycorn" jumps up,* |
| But he lived to tell the tale: | *very much alive, and reaches* |
| For they pour him out of an old brown jug | *out to grab a large brown earthenware jug, with which* |
| | *he pretends to fill the* |
| And they call him home brewed ale: | *glasses of all the children* |
| They call him home brewed ale. | *in the circle* |

The children picked up the song very rapidly, and (after some initial shyness) enjoyed acting it out. With each group of kids we repeated the whole song several times, since nearly everyone wanted a turn at being John Barleycorn.

*Sharing our faith with others* took place on the steps of the pulpit. The adult leader here was a member of our parish who is a priest with a deaf congregation. He taught the children the American

Sign Language signs for "I love you" and "Our Father," and spoke about his ministry with the deaf.

At the lectern was the *story* booth: a cart with books from our parish library and the public library. There were a couple of books actually about the eucharist or the Last Supper, several books on the Passover and on holiday celebrations in various traditions; books on wheat, grapes, bread, and wine; and picture books on family, community, and friendship, such as *The Relatives Came* by Cynthia Rylant, and *Friends* by Helme Heine. The book cart was attended by one adult, to read to its youngest visitors and chat in a relaxed way with older children as they browsed.

*A meal around a table* was the theme at the altar. A member of the altar guild had spread out a display of altar linens and silver, candles and vestments. Children were encouraged to touch and handle the objects, and ask questions: the leader did not explain the items one by one but let the children take the lead.

This booth was intended to operate as a foil to the first one. We had expected that the display of sacred vessels, snowy linens and opulent vestments, attractively displayed at the high altar, would exert a powerful attraction for children and that they would be eager to come close and handle them. Instead, we have found every year that this has been the least attended of all the booths. Adding incense one year increased involvement somewhat, but it was not the kind of involvement we wanted: the children's interest was primarily in playing with the matches and charcoal, giggling about the smell, and hoping the whole thing would explode.

Last year, on a whim, we added to the altar display the dollhouse-sized eucharist set from our Good Shepherd nursery: table, chalice, paten, priest, and eight little people. To our astonishment, the children responded with great intensity to these little figures, arranging and rearranging them around the altar, picking up and breaking the soft plasticine "loaf" on the paten, narrating the liturgy, discussing with the adult in charge such questions as whether the people should sit in straight rows or stand in a circle. The leader was then able to engage the children also with the real, life-size vessels.

After an hour, the children had had enough time to visit each booth for as long as any of them wanted. The next section, from 4:30 to 5:30, was spent in preparation for the offertory, or the *praying and sharing* section of the liturgy. The children divided into three groups: one prepared the bread and one the wine, while the third decorated simple green chasubles and stoles for our two priests.

The bread group made not only eucharistic bread but also a splendid large loaf in the shape of a sheaf of grain, to serve at the supper. The wine group filled a plastic tub with red grapes and took turns treading them into juice (to our surprise, the juice was delicious!)—like the bread, the "wine" was to be served with supper, while some was set aside to be consecrated in the eucharist. The vestments were decorated with wheat and grape designs created by carving simple shapes from the cut surfaces of potatoes and stamping them on the fabric with poster paint. The ink had not quite dried by supper, but the priests were good sports.

These activities all occurred in adjacent spaces, and after their experience with the Corpus Christi Fair, the children wanted to move freely between them. Though this had not been part of our plan, we gave up resisting it, and before long all the kids had juice-stained legs and paint-stained arms and were having a wonderful time.

In later years we have replaced the vestment decorating activity with mural painting, using powdered tempera (mixed ahead of time, by adults, in covered yoghurt cups, in a wide range of colors, with a separate brush for each color). We use 4-foot by 4-foot plywood panels, pre-primed, and laid on the floor over plenty of newspaper. The theme of "the Body of Christ" has inspired panels showing our church building surrounded by city, hills, and sky; spectacular depictions of the sacraments of baptism and eucharist; and a scene of the natural order—mountains, forests, desert, ocean, sky—all cradled in the large and loving hands of God.

From 5:30 to 6:00 we cleaned up, set the tables for supper, let the kids run around a little, and then relaxed with a couple of books from the book wagon as we waited for the parents to arrive. The tables were set in a long "U" shape, with tablecloths, candles, and flowers; at the end of the "U," the altar from the children's worship space made a fourth side and was furnished with frontal, candles, cross, and flowers. We wanted to make a parallel between the supper table and the altar, but not to identify them: we felt that if this eucharist was to connect in their minds with our Sunday morning eucharistic worship, it should happen at an altar rather than simply at the dinner table.

The celebration bulletin board had been brought in, and as the children's families arrived, we spent about ten minutes looking over it together, and adding to it some simple drawings by the parents, reflecting their own concerns for thanksgiving and intercessory prayer. Then, moving from *praying and sharing* to *breaking bread*, we sang a blessing and sat down to eat. Our clergy, a husband-and-wife team, presided as mother and father at this family meal as we talked of what we had done today, of family celebrations, joys and sorrows, and the special foods that each of us had brought.

As the meal finished, one of the priests read John 6:35, 50-51 (the Bread of Life) and the other read John 12:24-26 ("unless a grain of wheat falls into the ground and dies"), and a group of children performed the John Barleycorn dance. The priests spoke briefly about the Last Supper and Jesus' death and new life; then they rose from the table, putting on their newly decorated vestments and setting out on the altar the bread and "wine" that the children had made. Gathering their comments into a preface and Great Thanksgiving, the celebrants offered the bread and wine, which were shared from hand to hand along the tables: parents gave communion to their children, or children to their parents, as the order happened to fall. As the remaining fragments of the loaf were returned to the altar, we sang the doxology and got up to share the peace, to relax together, gather up our tired children, and *go out.*

It had been a long and rather sweaty afternoon. Between grapes and paint, pizza and chocolate frosting, I have never seen such grubby communicants in my whole life. But as all parents know, a dirty kid is a happy kid, and there was no mistaking the joy with which we took leave of each other. These children had been engaged in living out our eucharistic theology: in offering the work of their hands, in making and sharing food, in establishing deep and vital bonds with their parish family, and in approaching with their imaginations the mystery of sacrifice, resurrection, and thanksgiving. They were ready to go forth in peace, rejoicing in the power of the Spirit.

# NOTES

1. See Gretchen Wolff Pritchard, *Alleluia! Amen: The Sunday Paper's Communion Book for Children* (New Haven: The Sunday Paper, 1984).

2. *The Tale of John Barleycorn*, illus. Mary Azarian (Boston: David R. Godine, 1982).

3. The melody printed in Azarian's book is not a very appealing tune. The most singable version I've found, with a "fa la la" refrain and simpler lyrics, is recorded by the British group Steeleye Span, in their album *Below the Salt* (Chrysalis Records CHR 1008).

# Chapter 17

# The Celestial City

EVERAL YEARS AGO, leafing through a film catalog, I spotted an ad for *Dangerous Journey*, a film adaptation of Bunyan's classic, *The Pilgrim's Progress*. I was intrigued: the illustrations in the ad were beautifully done, in a fluid, traditional pen-and-ink style, with superb, confident draftsmanship, subtle watercolor, and bold composition. One showed Christian in rags, reading his book, with a huge, awkward burden weighing him down, and in the background, under a rolling, ominous East Anglian sky, the huddled roofs and pointed spires of an English town. In the other, Christian is pounding on the oak beams of the wicket gate, while arrows thud into the wood all around him. *Great* pictures, I thought, and made a mental note to investigate the series further. Our annual intergenerational Lenten program had a tradition of using films or readers' theater, and this began to look like a possibility for it.[1]

It is embarrassing for a Yale Ph.D. in English to confess it, but I never could get through *Pilgrim's Progress*. My first exposure to it was in third grade; my family had newly arrived in England and I was struggling with a new school, new customs, and a new pronunciation of the English language. The headmistress read *Pilgrim's Progress* aloud at morning prayers, day after day. She lost me almost at once. I thought the "great burden" on Christian's back was a great *burn*, and the "wicket gate" left me totally confused: it sounded like "wicked gate." The whole thing reeked of foreignness and mystification. I did absorb enough to catch the allusions when I later read *Little Women*, but Bunyan's original remained a closed book. As a college student I tried again—after all, this was, next to the Bible itself, the most read, most influential book in the English language, at least until Dr. Spock came along. But the allegorical characters failed to come to life; the seventeenth-century polemics dragged it all down; it all seemed dated, introverted, morbid, and recherché. If I'd had to read it for class, no doubt I would have overcome those obstacles and made my way into Bunyan's world, but as recreational reading—forget it.

Not long after I saw the ad for *Dangerous Journey*, I found a book version at a conference book table, bought it for the church library, and brought it home. As an experiment, I sat down with my children, then eight and four, and began the first chapter. They would not let me stop till the story was finished. What a contrast to my own introduction to the same story! And it *is* the same story. Some anti-Roman allegory is omitted; otherwise, the characters, episodes, and issues follow Bunyan exactly. Many of his phrases are retained verbatim. There remains a strong seventeenth-century flavor, but it is no longer a barrier to understanding. It is mostly the extremely powerful visualization of the characters and places that makes the difference. One can now go back to the original, unedited Bunyan, and read it through with excitement and absorption at last, because the emotionally telling visual images of the illustrator do not fade.

I talked the rector into letting us use the film version of *Dangerous Journey* as the Lenten program. The program was in the church undercroft, a large space, so we rented the 16-mm movies. They are not "animated" in the usual sense of the word: the characters do not move. Instead, the camera plays over the book's many illustrations, while a single narrator, Paul Copley, tells the story and speaks all the parts. His voice is flexible, rich, warm, and inviting; his mellow Yorkshire accent causes no serious comprehension problems. The musical accompaniment and sound effects are understated and always apt: in the first episode, especially, the wide, rolling landscapes and huge skies are brought to life by a faint, pastoral, poignant theme that opens up waves of longing in the viewer, giving great psychological depth to the story of Christian's yearning for the Celestial City.

What makes *Dangerous Journey* so refreshing among religious media for children is that it lets the story tell itself. It is about morality, certainly, but it does not come on with glib formulas or sweet little fables about love and sharing conquering all. Instead, it shows that the life of faith is a *struggle*; and this is so true to the actual experience of adult and child alike, and so rarely said nowadays in parish education settings, that it comes as a liberating revelation. Further (and even rarer today), it represents *the goal at the end of the quest as an object of openly acknowledged desire*, and as a thing of heart-stopping beauty. Through artwork, narration, and soundtrack it gives an authentic and deeply moving glimpse of that beauty that is not easily forgotten.

We have used *Dangerous Journey* twice, in two successive Lenten programs. The first year it was the focus for an intergenerational program, with a weekly potluck supper, movie, activities, and worship. We found that some families were leaving after the film, without participating in the activities, so for the final two sessions we did the activities first, before dinner. Even so, while children plunged happily in, adults tended to hang back.

The first week, we offered a choice: children or adults could work together to paint a large empty tomb on a huge piece of corrugated cardboard, or they could construct out of whatever furniture or materials they could find in the room, an obstacle course representing Christian's journey so far. The tomb referred to the moment in the story when Christian's burden rolls off his back into the open tomb of Christ; the painting the children made, with a hole cut at the doorway, has since been used many times in children's liturgies and play in the parish. That night we ran overtime, because once the obstacle course was finished every child in the place insisted on going through it individually, complete with a "burden" made of a backpack full of books.

The second week, we held a hymn sing, using some of the many hymns whose imagery draws on *Pilgrim's Progress*. An added bonus of learning *Pilgrim's Progress* is the fact that it clues one in to a whole literary tradition and vocabulary: "Apollyon," "Emmanuel's Ground," "Beulah Land," all are now characters or places that we know, instead of mysterious references in arcane evangelical hymns. The signature tune of the series, by the way, is "Monk's Gate," known by every British schoolchild as the proper tune of "He Who Would Valiant Be," Percy Dearmer's reworking of a Bunyan lyric. It's a grand tune and children love it, but the masculine language pervading the hymn may be offensive to some.

The third and fourth weeks, we made a giant map of Christian's whole journey. Cutting pictures from magazines and catalogs, we embellished the landmarks in the journey; the third week, Vanity Fair got special attention as we pasted up cutouts from advertisements for cars, hot tubs, and designer jeans. On the last week, we made paper figures of ourselves and placed them at any points on Christian's itinerary we felt we had also visited: the Slough of Despond, Doubting Castle, the Palace Beautiful (from which Christian has a vision of the Celestial City and is armed and refreshed by experienced disciples), the Valley of the Shadow of Death. As a conclusion, we marched upstairs to the chapel, singing "Marching to Zion" (*Lift Every Voice and Sing*, Hymn 92). The children especially took this rousing hymn to heart at once. We ended with a eucharist—a foretaste of the Celestial City.

The following year, the Lenten series was moved to Sunday morning after church, with separate programs for adults and children. We used *Dangerous Journey* a second time, because there had been a near-complete turnover in the church school enrollment. Originally conceived as a "babysitting" activity to occupy children while their parents stayed for the adult program, the series became instead a specific drawing card for children (some even showed up after having missed church) and parents found themselves constrained to stay for the adult program because their children insisted on going to the film series.

In this more intimate setting, we borrowed a VCR each week and bought the videos of *Dangerous Journey* (buying videos is hardly more expensive than renting 16-mm movies). Each week, the children watched two chapters of the story, and then worked on hand puppets with papier maché heads. By the third week, they were asked to choose a character from the story (by then, most of the characters had been introduced) for their puppet to represent. They painted the heads; I took the puppets home and sewed bodies for them, and the fourth week, they decorated the bodies. It was then that several children remarked, "All the good guys in the story have plain clothes; all the bad guys have fancy, lacy, fussy clothes."

On the fifth and final week, the children had half an hour to develop and rehearse a puppet show to present to the adults. It was a week since they had seen the last episode and four weeks since the first. Yet they all had near-total recall of every character and scene—much better than the adults who had undertaken to lead them and narrate their show. They did a marvelous show, full of life, passion, and humor. I like to think that Bunyan would have been pleased.

# NOTES

1. *Dangerous Journey*, illus. Allan Parry (Grand Rapids: Eerdmans, 1990). A film/video adaptation is available from Gateway Films/Vision Video, 2030 Wentz Church Road, Worcester, PA 19490 (telephone 800-523-0226).

# Chapter 18

# Three Kings' Saturday

THE FEAST OF EPIPHANY on January 6 celebrates the visit of the magi to the infant Jesus, while the Sunday after Epiphany is reserved for the Baptism of our Lord. Except when January 6 falls on a Sunday, the celebration of the three kings is likely either to be collapsed back into the Christmas Sundays or to disappear entirely. This is regrettable not only because the feast is a splendidly colorful one with enormous appeal to children, but also because it is a major part of the heritage of our Hispanic brothers and sisters. The occasion last year of the bishop's visit for baptism and confirmation on Epiphany 2 led us to think creatively how we could prepare three first-graders—one of them Hispanic—for baptism, in the context of the three kings aspect of the Feast of Epiphany, the baptismal focus of Epiphany 1, and the bishop's visit.

Epiphany is a feast of light, which gave extra meaning to our regular custom of decorating candles for baptismal candidates. We did this together while the children were arriving and settling in, starting at 10:00 a.m. We used beeswax altar candles—about 10 inches high and $1\frac{1}{2}$ inches thick—and decorated them with shapes cut out of colored sheets of beeswax, which are simply pressed onto the candle.[1]

About a dozen of our forty-odd Sunday school children showed up, mostly in the four-to-eight age range; this was a low-key event, focused more on keeping company with the baptismal candidates than on communally observing the Epiphany festival. When all were settled in, we reviewed the story of salvation. I used a large homemade flannelboard and felt cutouts to reinforce the story, which briefly narrates "God's Saving Work" from Creation and Fall through the Flood and Exodus, the promised land, and the life, death, and resurrection of Jesus, and ends by affirming that through baptism we become part of all the saving things that God has done.

The flannelboard is simply a sheet of plywood, about 3 by 4 feet in size, with royal blue flannel stretched across its surface and stapled down on the reverse side. Instead of the extremely realistic flannel figures that are featured in Sunday school supply catalogs, I use large, brightly colored felt symbols, many of which appear repeatedly in slightly different contexts, suggesting parallels and connections between different parts of the story. Given half a chance, the children always play with the pieces afterward. Freely rearranging the symbols, experimenting with the meanings these arrangements suggest, they become theologians. Watching this happen is one of the joys of using this technique.

To tell the story, I used the following felt symbols:

- Two hands and a heart, for God
- A red/orange/yellow burst of light
- A large white dove, with cruciform halo
- About a dozen blue ripples, for water
- About a dozen small colored fish, and a few pieces of green sea weed
- An Apple tree with a snake twining round it
- Adam and Eve (tan male and female silhouettes)
- Ark (silhouette)
- Noah and a few animals (optional; the animals, if used, should first be used as part of the creation story)
- Raindrops (also used in the baptism sequence)
- Tiny dove to go in the sky above the ark
- Rainbow
- Pillar of cloud (becomes the pillar of fire by having the burst of light added)
- About a dozen small human figures—just white robes with

brown heads—to cross the Red Sea
- Several small fruit trees to represent the promised land
- Manger, with baby to go in it (naked silhouette in fetal position)
- Star (should resemble burst of light)
- Figure of Jesus, arms extended, wearing loincloth only
- Medium-sized white dove with halo
- Buff-colored robe to put on Jesus
- Cross to fit behind Jesus figure
- Large whale (one of the human figures from the Exodus goes inside it as Jonah)
- Church (should resemble the ark—put people in it and a dove over it)
- Font, in silhouette: baby figure goes in it, raindrops over it; also dove over it
- Paschal candle, to be capped with same burst of light as pillar of fire

The children "helped" me put up the shapes, providing many suggestions and comments about how they should be placed.

The three kings part of the day was the Jesse Tree Treasure Hunt in the church. We crowned the three baptismal candidates as the three kings, and handed out ten numbered, sealed envelopes to the rest of the children at random. The child receiving envelope number 1 was designated as the Star, and carried a gold star in procession to lead the kings into the church. There the first envelope was opened, and its contents read:

God made the earth, the sun and stars
God made the planets too;
The animals, the birds and fish
And God made me and you.

God's Spirit on the waters deep
Made life begin to move;
God's Spirit fills us with new life
And teaches us to love.

We come to church to share that life,
That love that makes us grow;
Look for your first gift near the door
Where people come and go.

The Star was responsible for leading the "kings" to the place suggested by the clue, finding the treasure, and taking it to the tree. The first treasure, hidden near the main doors, was a small Christmas tree ornament in the form of a dove. Then the processional star was passed to the child holding envelope number 2, which read:

> God made a man and woman
> And gave them life and breath;
> God told them "Do not touch that tree,
> For it will bring you death."
>
> The serpent said, "Oh no it won't,
> It's sure to make you wise."
> The man and woman listened
> Though the snake was telling lies.
>
> They went and ate the apple
> They wanted to be smart.
> But pain and shame and sorrow
> Came instead into their hearts.
>
> Their story in the Bible
> Is the story of us all.
> We need to listen to God's word
> We need to hear his call.
>
> On Sundays when the preacher
> Stands up to preach the Word
> The people sit and listen
> So God's message can be heard.
>
> Look in the place for preachers,
> Find a fruit there for your tree,
> And may the Spirit give you life
> And Jesus set you free.

This ornament was an apple, and was found, of course, in the pulpit. Envelope 3 read:

> The world was very wicked
> And God was very sad,
> Because the people everywhere
> Were doing what was bad.

God made it rain for forty days
To wash the world of sin;
But God told Noah, "Make an ark
And bring the creatures in."

So Noah and his family
And creatures two by two
Were saved from drowning in the flood
And filled the world anew.

God drowns our sins in water
When we're baptized in his Name.
Look where the water comes from
And you'll find it's still the same.

In the font was found a miniature Noah's ark. (Our family happens to have such a Christmas tree ornament, but if you can't find an ornament you can simply draw the ark, cut it out, and put a hook on it.)

For number 4:

There was a man named Abraham
And Sarah was his wife.
God made from them a people
Who would lead us to new life.

Three angels came to Abraham
And said, "You'll have a son."
And he believed God's promise
And said, "God's will be done."

Abraham and Sarah
Led the way in faith and prayer.
Look where the priest, our leader, sits
And find a treasure there.

On the seat of the rector's stall in the chancel was an angel ornament. The fifth treasure was a lamb ornament, found on the altar via the following clue:

God's people down in Egypt
Cried out in slavery,
And God told Moses, "It is time
To set my people free."

The night was dark and gloomy,
The people shook with fear,
For Egypt's mighty army
Was getting very near.

But Moses told the people
"Your God will save you yet,"
And they walked right through the ocean
Without even getting wet.

On the night when they left Egypt
The people ate their bread;
They killed a lamb and roasted it
Right before they fled.

The Lamb of God is Jesus
His blood will set us free
We eat the bread and drink the wine
And sing of victory.

Look where the bread is broken
And where the wine is poured,
And find the Lamb of God who died
And is our living Lord.

The sixth treasure was hidden at the base of the large brass cross on the former high altar, past the choir stalls. It was a tiny perfume bottle filled with olive oil:

God's people came to Israel
And there they settled down,
And there they chose as leader
A king who wears a crown.

His name was little David.
He was a shepherd boy.
He sang and played upon the harp
And filled their hearts with joy.

When people chose a leader
They poured upon his head
The holy oil of gladness:
"You are our King," they said.

Look way up in the front
Where the happy voices ring
And find the oil of gladness
By the cross of Christ, our King.

Our lectern is in the shape of an eagle. On the eagle's shoulder
was a tiny brass trumpet, and this was its clue:

"Thus speaks the God of Israel,"
The holy prophets said.
God's word was spoken loud and clear
For the people that they led.

"What does the Lord require of you?
Love mercy, live in peace.
God saves, forgives, and loves you,
And his Kingdom will increase."

Look where the Eagle stands
For the swiftly-flying Word
And find the sign of prophets
Who call us to our Lord.

The eighth clue led to the Christmas creche that was set up at
the base of the altar. In it were hidden the Mary and Joseph figures
from a much smaller nativity scene:

After many years of waiting
Israel received her King:
The Lord was born in Bethlehem,
They heard the angels sing.

The mother's name was Mary
As the holy Scriptures tell;
And Joseph was her husband,
And the child—Emmanuel.

Look in the lowly stable
With the shepherds standing by
And find the parents of the Lord
Who sang his lullabye.

Perpendicular to the main church is our small Lady Chapel,
with lovely stained glass windows portraying Jesus' infancy. One of

them shows the three kings, and on the windowsill there was a bowl of gold foil, a flagon of real incense, and a jar of myrrh:

Three Kings from distant places
Came following a Star;
To find the King of Heaven
They traveled very far.

Now you must make a journey
To a different holy place,
And there in glowing windows
You will see the baby's face.

Where the Kings present their treasures
You will find those treasures too:
Gold, and myrrh, and precious incense
For the Lord who came to you.

The last treasures were a collection of blank sheets of paper, mounted on red or green cardboard and threaded with lengths of yarn to hang them from the tree. They were hidden under the cushions of the communion rail, along with a supply of felt markers:

The journey now is over,
For the Lord has come to earth
And the Kings have found his cradle
And celebrate his birth.

But the story is not finished
For God's work is never done,
And as he called the Wise Men
So he calls us every one.

We are called to be his people
And we come from every place
To share his blood and body
And give thanks for all his grace.

In the place where bread is given
And the holy cup is passed
You will find a gift to offer,
And it is the very last:

For this gift will tell a story—
A story that is true:
The story of God's calling
Of a special person—YOU.

On the cards the children were asked to draw a picture of a time when they felt especially close to God; these were also hung on the tree.

The treasure hunt was enthusiastically received—too much so, in fact, as the children reading clues were drowned out by many voices guessing the treasure's hiding place, and as soon as the place was guessed, the whole crowd would take off at a run and turn up the treasure, leaving the Star, who was supposed to ceremoniously lead the kings, still struggling with the hard words in the clue. If we do it again we will have adults read the clues: they will read louder, more clearly, and with more authority. We will also establish from the start the principle that nobody *goes* to where the treasure is thought to be until all have *decided together* where to go, and *the Star is the leader and is the one who will actually uncover the gift.* If you use these little rhymes you may need to fiddle with numbers 7 and 9, which refer to our eagle lectern and to our stained glass windows in a "different holy place" (the Lady Chapel); and perhaps also with number 6, if your chancel lacks choir stalls and high altar.

We made no particular effort, on this occasion, to introduce Hispanic flavor into what we were doing; we had too little time and, as I have mentioned, the agenda was baptismal rather than seasonally festive. If the kids' attention span had allowed it, we were going to make collages after lunch on the themes of light and dark, water and wind. This never happened; in fact the day never really regained focus after the treasure hunt. Plans to draw the Sunday congregation's attention to the Jesse Tree also fell through the cracks, but we did manage to incorporate the baptismal candidates into the procession of the costumed three kings that (most unrubrically) launched the liturgy on Epiphany 1, the next morning. And several weeks later, I spotted Kelly, one of the children we had baptized, carefully explaining every one of the ornaments on the tree to a friend.

The Jesse Tree is usually associated with Advent, and our treasure hunt would also work as an Advent activity. But by associating the tree not so much with the *ancestors of Christ* as with the *story of salvation*, and presenting the story as a *journey* or a *quest*, we were able to link two aspects of Epiphany that usually are barely on speaking terms: the three kings and the baptismal mystery. Held at night, as a family party, the same activities could culminate in a eucharist emphasizing the theme of light, another baptismal theme. The work of incarnating scriptural and liturgical themes to give them real imaginative power for children is so exciting in large part because of the way the themes come to life—not in isolation, as curricular elements skillfully communicated to children, but in real dialogue: many voices speaking the same Good News, many different roads pointing to Jerusalem.

# NOTES

1. The wax is made in Germany by a company named Stockmar. It is available in art stores or may be ordered through the *Hearthsong* catalog (P.O. Box B, Sebastopol, CA 95473; 800-325-2502).

2. *New Life: The Sunday Paper's Baptism Book* (New Haven: The Sunday Paper, 1986).

Part Four

# Out of the Basement

*Children In the Worshiping Community*

# Chapter 19

# Out of the Basement

I N 1 9 6 9, A S A sophomore in college, I decided I wanted to teach Sunday school. I called the parish office, and was put in touch with the assistant, a young man a couple of years out of seminary who had just arrived that summer. He was thrilled to hear that I wanted to teach. He assigned me to the second grade, showed me where the classroom and the supply cabinet were, and turned me loose.

I knew nothing about second graders. I had no curriculum. I had been in the parish less than a year, and I knew none of the children and none of their parents. I had no idea what they had done in their previous year of church school; the classes were held in separate rooms, and I never met the other teachers. No one came and watched my class, or asked how I was doing. If they had, they would have seen me talking way over the heads of a half-dozen bored and confused seven-year-olds; it never dawned on me, all year, that teaching primary children might require different methods than the college-style lecture and "discussion" I was using. I did keep order in the classroom, more or less. But what most terrifies me, looking back, is that one or two of the parents sought me out, and told me what a pleasure it was to have a decent teacher for a change.

I wish I could say I thought this experience was atypical, or that things had gotten a lot better since 1969. But my experience was much the same at the next parish to which I took my enthusiasm for Sunday school teaching. The Sunday school was run by the seminarian, a different person each year. There was no curriculum. Teachers did what they could with what materials they could find or make up. The occasional energetic volunteer who tried to provide organization and direction soon burned out. The space, in the basement, was dingy, cluttered, unsuitable for its purpose, and unsafe. And I have heard the same story, again and again, from all across the church.

The canons of the Episcopal Church require that lectors and chalice-bearers must be trained and officially enrolled or even licensed by the bishop. These ministries are simple, mechanical tasks, requiring minimal talent or training, but we care enough about the dignity of our liturgy and the holiness of word and sacrament to make sure that they are performed with skill and grace. But anyone can walk in off the street and teach Sunday school. No training is required, no license is conferred, no recognition is given. Church school teachers do their work anonymously, in the back hall or basement. Once the annual quota of volunteers has been filled, the congregation (and often the clergy), with a sigh of relief, happily hand over to them the whole business and do their best to forget about it for the rest of the year.

The Book of Common Prayer provides prayers for everything from the anniversary of the dedication of a church to "mission," "the ministry," and "education," but none for *Christian* education. Apparently the idea that a parish, deanery, or diocese might hold a liturgy celebrating or supporting or offering up its work of teaching children never entered the minds of the compilers. Years go by in some dioceses without a single workshop for teachers; fewer than half of all dioceses, nationwide, have a staff position for Christian education. I know of at least one diocese that has an annual retreat and conference for liturgical assistants, but no comparable event for Sunday school teachers.

Episcopalians have the sound and laudable conviction that liturgy is important, that worship is central, that the way we pray in community is what really forms our faith, kindles our hope, fuels our love. We formulate the words of our worship with great care;

we pay serious attention to the effect of its gestures, movement, music, and images on our conscious and subconscious imaginations. In our eucharistic liturgy, we gather in a special place, set aside and adorned for sacred and holy purposes. We are invited to approach with awe and love the One who made us, guides us, loves and feeds us. We are encouraged to fantasize, to role-play, to listen to stories full of powerful images, to sing, to embrace, to confess, to adore, to be changed, to be fed, to be sent out.

Meanwhile, where are the children?

More often than not, the children are in a classroom, not a sacred space—a classroom, moreover, that is likely to be small, unattractive, and untidy. They are in a world of academic, workaday norms and behaviors. Leaving them to do their fantasizing, pretending, wondering, and loving in their weekday lives, we bring them to church to sit them down with an academic curriculum or, perhaps, to engage in craft activities or simplified liturgies whose bottom line is often a moral lesson or a "right answer." We give them little chance to experience on a deep level the most vital subject-matter of our faith: its concern with loss and guilt, with sacrifice and suffering, with reconciliation, restoration, and resurrection. Even the most basic act of worship, participation in the eucharist, is usually closed to children until they have first studied it in the communion preparation class.

The nurture of children within the parish is commonly known as "Christian education," and takes place almost exclusively through a parish structure known as the "Sunday school," which models itself on regular school. It is organized in *classes*, with *teachers*, who use *curriculums*, with *lesson plans*. It operates on the unspoken assumption that children must learn how to be Christians, in an academic setting, before they can actually begin to do any of the things that Christians normally do together in the community of faith: pray together, celebrate the sacraments, share their faith and their lives, cherish the hope of things unseen, and bear witness in love and service in the world. And in Episcopal churches, the usual time for Sunday school is *during* the time of the main worship service. Adults come to church on Sunday in or-

der to worship; children come to Sunday school to acquire information.

Children are also often forgotten as the parish goes about its
work in the local community and the world. They may participate
in a service project—making something for a parish fair, adopting a
child overseas, singing carols at an old people's home—but again,
this activity usually serves as a class project. The children participate as a learning experience for them, in a class group, rather
than because they, as parish members along with their own families, have something to offer to meet a human need out of love for
God.

Christian education is no substitute for real, living membership
in the community of faith. That does not make it unimportant. It
is vital that children (as well as adults) learn to use the Bible and
the vocabulary of our faith, to understand that there is real intellectual meat on the bones of the creeds, that the gospel challenges
them on every level of their minds as well as their hearts and their
hands and their whole lives. But the Episcopal Church, after a
burst of enthusiasm in the 1950s, has given little attention to serious Christian education for any age group. Issues of liturgy,
church order, and social witness have occupied nearly all its energies. It can be argued that *adult* education does go on in the liturgy, if the liturgy is well done and the sermon is substantial. But
the church has continued to segregate children from the worshiping community where its own life is most richly lived. And at the
same time it has, as an institution, shown an appalling indifference
to their needs even within the confines of the academic classroom.

Alone among mainline denominations, the Episcopal Church
operates no publishing house, and publishes no curriculums for
Sunday schools. Curriculum materials aimed at the Episcopal mar-
ket are available from a variety of sources, ranging from large publishing houses to individual entrepreneurs, and there have been
several impressive new developments in this area in the last several
years. But there are still, as of this writing, no published curriculum materials from any source that are officially endorsed by the
national church, or evaluated or abstracted—or even listed—for the

help of the parish educator. General Convention must authorize a new translation of Scripture before it can be read aloud in the liturgy for adults, but it is all one to the national church whether the children are using a curriculum from some other denomination, or a curriculum with dubious theology, ecclesiology, or methodology, or even, as is very often the case, whether the teachers (untrained, unlicensed, unsupervised) are making up their own lessons from week to week. The church exerts no effort to suggest that by a certain age children should have mastered, or at least been exposed to, certain bodies of material in a certain sequence; the church offers no norm against which to judge the effectiveness of one's local program.

Almost every lay ministry in the parish has more dignity than that of Sunday school teacher—and more support from the national and diocesan organization. Episcopal parish educators need help: help in identifying and choosing materials, in recruiting and training teachers, in leadership development and teaching techniques, in networking and sharing ideas and discoveries, in our own continuing Christian education and spiritual growth. We need workshops. We need bibliographies. We need space to be regularly devoted to our concerns in the general publications of the church at all levels. *We need the church to seek us out:* most of us are volunteers with neither the time nor the training to hunt down the few helps the church does make available.

Within the parish, we need to know that our work, and those we work with, are considered valuable and important by and in the Body of Christ. We need to be visible. We need to be held up and prayed for and celebrated. We need to have the needs of children, families, and teachers factored into decisions about parish life and parish programs. *We need time:* more time in class with the children, and a Sunday morning schedule that makes it possible for the rector to visit the Sunday school at least occasionally, and does not require teachers and children to be absent week after week from the Sunday liturgy.

Teachers who are kept from the liturgy are prime candidates for burnout. Children who are kept from the liturgy are learning that

142

the parish is not an inclusive community but an adult club: that its sacred space is for grown-ups only; that its normative rituals need to be mediated through adult patterns of understanding before they can be experienced, or else must be watered down into kiddie versions; that the gospel message is somehow different for children and adults.

Baptized children are not recruits or trainees. They are Christians. It is their birthright as Christians to be included in the life of God's people in community: to approach God in awe and love in worship, to be welcomed into the sacred space, to receive Christ's Body and Blood, to know and be known to their fellow-parishioners by name, and to express their faith in service, not as a class exercise only, but as members of the parish family. Children must not be excluded from worship, even if that means that they spend less time in class because their parents will not bring them to a class at any other time. We need to rethink what we mean by Christian education, and rearrange many of our parish structures.

The nurture of children in the parish is much more than Christian education. Children learn by watching and imitating adults, and by projecting themselves into imaginary worlds. Our liturgy, with its rich admixture of verbal and non-verbal, of colors and sounds and smells and gestures, is the primary source of nourishment for our adults, and should also nourish our children. But if this is to happen, clergy and worship committees must give serious thought to making the Sunday worship truly accessible to children, and educating parents and other parishioners to see children as fellow-worshipers, not as intruders who have to be hushed or distracted so that adults are left free to pray.

For parents, especially, accepting children as fellow-worshipers means learning new ways of interacting with them in church. Instead of saying "Shhhhh!!!" or offering a cracker or a bottle or a storybook (even a Bible storybook), we parents will need to learn to invite our children to experience the liturgy with us, on their own level. We will need to learn to sit right in front, where children can see, and to pick up a restless child, and gently whisper in his ear, "Look, do you see the priest? What is she doing? Listen, now she's going to say some special words that Jesus said...See, now she's picking up the cup...."

Accepting children as fellow-worshipers means accepting the responsibility we undertook at the baptism of each child in our parish, to do all in our power to support this child in his or her new life in Christ. In a very real sense, we are all godparents of every child in our parish. This responsibility may mean, for instance, that we take turns, from week to week, sitting with a particularly restless child so that the parents of that child can worship in peace. We remain committed to the child's being there with us before God's altar, but we recognize the parents' need to stand undistracted before God as well—not only for their own sakes but ultimately for the child's sake also.

Children belong in the worshiping community. But that does not mean that the Sunday school is passé, and we can now neglect the classroom with a clear conscience. The claim that children belong in church, and the equally unassailable claim that parents are the primary nurturers of their children's faith, can serve as excuses for the parish's continued failure (in either classroom or sanctuary) to nurture children's faith in ways that are truly accessible to them. Such reasoning also reflects a massive disregard for the many children who show up in church without their parents' active interest and support, and who hunger for the gospel and for Christian community all the more for that reason.

If the Sunday liturgy alone is to engage the children with the gospel, our forms of worship will have to change much more than they have. If parents are to do all the instruction in the children's religious training, they will have to get a lot more pastoral help than they are getting now. In the meantime, children need the gospel to be preached to them right now, or their participation in the sacraments will indeed become the sentimental charade that its critics are calling it.

The Sunday morning class will continue to have an important role to play. But it is increasingly inappropriate as the normative setting for the parish's nurture of children. This does not mean we cut out "Christian education." It means we find creative new structures for it—structures that have emerged out of the basement and become less segregated from liturgy and from children's imaginative and emotional lives. There may be other times than Sunday morning when parents will prove willing to bring their children to class. A vacation Bible school, or several Saturday workshops spaced throughout the year, offer opportunities for longer hours of time together, more experiential learning in mixed age groups, and forms of worship that children can enter into with enthusiasm and understanding. Drama—not only the traditional Christmas pageant but also mime, puppetry, and scriptural role-playing—can walk the fine and very exciting line between liturgy and learning. Rather than learning in class *about* such powerful Christian symbols as bread, children can come to realize that every time they come together for a Saturday workshop, one of the activities is bread baking—and the bread thus baked always appears on the altar the next morning. They can come to know things in their very bones, not only with their heads. And, as we all know, that is the kind of knowledge that takes hold, that lasts beyond the class and the workbook and the project, and becomes part of our deepest selves.

Jesus said, "Feed my sheep"; he also said, "Feed my lambs." Nowhere did he tell his disciples to feed the sheep, but only *teach* the lambs...and he certainly never told them to feed the sheep but keep the lambs down in the basement with untrained shepherds and a wretched supply of moldy hay or junk food. It is time for the Sunday school to come up out of the basement and for children and teachers to claim their place with the rest of their brothers and sisters in Christ. It is time for them to stand before God's altar in wonder and praise, to be included and respected as they affirm their faith, share their hope, and offer their love in service to the world.

# Chapter 20

# Which Curriculum?

WHAT ARE YOU LOOKING for your curriculum to do? Teach children the Bible? Develop their faith? Transmit to them the particular outlook, heritage, and lore of a specific tradition within the church? Help them to see their daily lives in the light of the gospel? Incorporate them into the worship life of the parish? Arm them against the encroachments of secular culture? Christian education materials currently available reflect a variety of different models of Christian nurture and its place in the life of the worshiping community. A parish undertaking to choose a curriculum needs to begin by examining its own understanding of Christian education and how it interacts with every aspect of parish life.

It may help to brainstorm some of your goals in a group—formulate them freely, let them be as sweeping or as specific as you like, and write them all down on a chalkboard or newsprint—then go over the list, rephrase and combine them where that seems appropriate, and rank them in order of importance to you in your parish. How much of a consensus do you find? Do teachers, parents, Christian education coordinator, and clergy share a similar outlook? Do you form into "parties," or is a whole range of perspectives represented? Where there is broad divergence of outlook but basic good will, a good compromise may be for different teachers to choose separate curriculums, rather than try to impose a single core curriculum on the parish education program as a whole. Care will need to be taken to prevent the church school from becoming a mere collection of individual teachers' agendas, but if well managed, such a scenario can offer children a refreshing variety of learning styles and spiritualities, and help them appreciate the breadth and diversity of the church's life.

Visit a resource center or order by mail the sample packets that most publishers provide for their curricular materials. Allow plenty of time for looking them over; note down your reactions. There are many different ways of considering a curriculum, and it may be of special interest to you to observe whether your questions or reactions as you actually look at the samples correspond to the terms in which you formulated your goals for Christian education in the parish. Do you find yourselves considering new and different issues, raised by the materials themselves? Now you will need to ask how important these new issues are: do they take precedence over your originally formulated concerns? You may need to go back and rework your original list, perhaps more than once.

Probably the most frequently cited concern for a curriculum is that it should be "Bible-centered." Parents and teachers alike join in formulating this goal. But once one looks at a few curriculums, one can see that the idea of "Bible-centered" can be understood in very different ways.

One curriculum begins with Genesis and works through the Bible in chronological order over a span of several years, giving at least some attention to every major story. Another proceeds in thematic units, keyed to the academic year and the church year and reflecting children's developmental levels, and illustrates these themes with carefully chosen biblical stories, characters, and quotations, gradually building up, in the course of several years, a fairly balanced (but unchronological) tour through the different eras of biblical history and the different types of biblical narrative. Another closely follows the three-year liturgical lectionary, focusing each week on at least one of the Scriptures read at the liturgy, and relying on the internal logic of the church's year to provide the framework and context. Still another rearranges the stories to fit children's developmental levels, but makes no reference to the church's year or even the school year: instead, it provides tape recordings and study questions for each child to complete individually at his or her own pace, so that no two members of the group are necessarily doing the same work at the same time.

Each of these curriculums is described by its publishers as "Bible-centered," but their use of the Bible is very different. In addition, some curriculums intentionally teach "biblical literacy," or the skill of finding one's way about the Bible, citing chapters and verses, listing scriptural characters and events, using maps and concordances, while others do not. Among those that do, such skills may be taught with a "fundamentalist" or a "historical-critical" orientation, or somewhere in between—or these issues may be sidestepped entirely and left to the teacher to deal with.

It should be clear by now that the way a curriculum responds to the imperative to be "Bible-centered" reflects an entire theology, often incompletely articulated, of the role of Scripture in forming individual and corporate faith. There is a world of difference in children's experience of the Scriptures within the Body of Christ, between a church school class consisting of individual listening stations with individual storybooks, workbook questions to answer, and an individual art project, each checked off on a tally sheet before beginning the next unit, and a class consisting of a circle of children gathered to hear the same gospel that the adults are hearing in church, and responding to it by singing, working together to make a banner, and then carrying that banner into church at the offertory.

Both of these models have been specifically drawn up for use in the Episcopal Church; both have been widely applied and widely hailed as "successful." Each has its advantages and disadvantages. But we are kidding ourselves if we think that they are merely two different ways of packaging the same product: Scripture, faith, and the life of the church. Taken in themselves, they are almost totally different. Obviously, a parish can greatly narrow the gap between these two approaches by what else we do with our time on Sunday morning: a lectionary curriculum may be much less integrated into the Sunday worship than this sketch suggests; an academic curriculum can be heavily supplemented. The difference, however, remains.

In the concern over the place of Scripture in Christian education, other areas of the church's life and experience may be forgotten entirely. Look back over your list of priorities: besides Scripture, what else did you want to make sure to offer your children? Some curriculums deliberately make a place for church history, lives of saints, units on church seasons, holidays, sacraments, theological concepts ("covenant" or "ministry," for example), and Christian ethics. Others do not, and parishes committed to including these topics in their children's nurture may have to supplement their main curriculum, or use a combination.

There are also some practical, less theological questions to ask of a curriculum. The realities of parish size and resources may cause these to override other considerations and point us toward some particular curriculum in spite of its imperfections in some areas. How large is your program? If you have only a dozen children, ranging in age from four to fourteen, there is little reason to look at a curriculum based on a fixed sequence of closely-graded levels from kindergarten to eighth grade. Conversely, a large parish with many children and little money has no hope of success with a curriculum based on the use of individual tape machines. Next, how much help does the curriculum give the teacher? Some teachers simply must have a lesson guide that gives step-by-step instructions not only for each project but for each class session; others will never follow instructions but will always go their own way, and may be happiest with a lesson plan consisting primarily of adult-level insights into the scriptural or other subject matter.

How about the suggested projects: are they varied enough to please children and teachers? Do they give children an opportunity to wonder, explore, and express their own response to the lesson material, or do they consist only of reproducing a standard model by exactly following instructions? Are they silly, cute, or irrelevant to the lesson material? Are they practical—do they match your talents and resources, and can they be carried out in the class time you have available? Give your teachers time to take a hard look at these considerations, and to express their reactions freely.

Finally, how does the curriculum "feel"? Is it faithful to the depth, complexity, and power of Scripture and Christian tradition, or does it give simplistic answers or none at all? How is the artwork? Is it patronizing, sensational, or technically poor, or does it invite a child into wonder and mystery? How about the figure of Jesus—is he blond and blue-eyed? Handsome, athletic, and always smiling? Are the pictures of daily life inclusive of different races, ages, sexes, and social conditions? Do the questions and stories respect children's experience? What is its "bottom line"—is the gospel subliminally equated with "being good" at home and school and being glad and thankful at church, and not much else? What about the format: is the type style attractive and the printing free of typographical errors? Do you catch any factual errors? Your teachers and children will be living with these materials; if they don't feel good, think hard about getting them, however well recommended they come.

A curriculum is a valuable tool in the parish's nurture of its children. No curriculum, by itself, can bring about sound and balanced Christian nurture; indeed, it is well not to think of parish nurture first of all in terms of the academic model that the term "curriculum" brings to mind. But a well-chosen curriculum, offered as part of a wider parish effort to include children in the worship and life of the church, can be instrumental in fostering faith and awakening devotion and conscience, as well as transmitting information. There are good materials out there. It is up to us to use them wisely and with creativity and love.

Chapter 21

# All God's Children

APARISH I KNOW—I'll call it St. David's—has a superb choir and a long tradition of Morning Prayer as the main Sunday morning service, two Sundays a month. All other things being equal, the rector would prefer to have the eucharist as the principal worship service every Sunday, but all other things aren't equal. The choir treasures the opportunity to offer its gifts to the congregation through choral Morning Prayer, with its stately, harmonious beauty, rooted in centuries of balanced, clear-eyed Anglican piety. Many in the congregation treasure the offering, and the rector knows this.

Last year, however, the rector and assistant were both approached by several families expressing deep frustration with the order of Morning Prayer, chiefly on account of their children. The children did not seem to appreciate the aesthetic strengths of Morning Prayer. They were bored and restless; furthermore, they were baffled and distressed that Sunday worship offered them the opportunity to take part in the eucharist only some of the time. The families asked that the eucharist be made available at a main service every Sunday, because that was the form of worship that held meaning for their children.

There was much deliberation. It was eventually decided to add another service on Morning Prayer Sundays. It would be a eucharist, held in the parish's capacious chapel at the same hour as

Morning Prayer. It would not be a "children's chapel" attended by children as a group while their parents went to the main service, nor even a "family service" which would seem, from its name, to discourage attendance by teenagers and individual adults. The planning committee chose a deliberately ambiguous name, "Service of Celebration," and carefully avoided emphasizing "family" or "children" in the advance notices of the new liturgy. But they agreed that the first consideration was the need of young families for liturgy that their children could find nourishing.

Why was choral Morning Prayer frustrating for children and their families? What was the lack that this new liturgy should be designed to address?

Obviously, there was the sacrament itself: children who regularly receive communion come to expect Sunday worship to meet them where they cannot fail to sit up and take notice: in their hands, their bodies, their mouths and stomachs. A child may sit through the entire service of Morning Prayer without once making contact with what the adults are doing, but that is impossible at the eucharist. Children know, of course, that the offering of food is a gift of love: "Take, eat, this is *for you.*" Even the smallest children learn to associate being in church with receiving this gift; when it is lacking, their worship experience remains unconsummated.

Then there is the movement involved in a normal parish eucharist—passing the peace, leaving one's seat to come forward for communion, to kneel, receive, and return—which is for children not only a welcome diversion but also a source of distinct landmarks in what is otherwise a trackless wilderness of words and music. Without such landmarks, children who can neither read nor tell time have no sense of how much of the liturgy has gone by. They react like kids on a long highway trip: after five minutes, they begin to whine, "Daddy, are we there yet?"

There is less to do at Morning Prayer than at the eucharist; there is also less to see, and even, for most children, less to listen to. Anthems and canticles of unpredictable length and with unintelligible words, sung from afar while the congregation merely listens, can convey a real sense of awe and transcendence—but, however well done, they did not seem to be doing this for the children at St. David's. The kids were not listening—did not want to listen. The parents' job on Morning Prayer Sundays was reduced to providing quiet diversions so that the children, while physically present, could amuse themselves without distracting the adults.

Those who were planning the Service of Celebration at St. David's had long been concerned with the behavior of children in church, but now they were approaching it in a new way—they were not asking, "How can we keep the children from disturbing us as we worship in ways that are dear to us?" but rather, "How can we invite children into real involvement with our worship of God? What is the essence of our worship and what is merely adult habit and prejudice? Can we make the whole liturgy accessible to children without losing the adults?" Asking these questions gave them a whole new perspective on what it is we do when we worship together.

If children were genuinely to participate, the space in the chapel, and the liturgy itself, must be arranged so they could see, move, and do things. Since the goal was that all ages would participate together, the service was not to be a rewritten, watered, or didactic liturgy, but an adaptation of Rite II, slightly simplified in vocabulary and syntax but without substantial alterations. There were to be as many opportunities as possible for children to contribute directly to the liturgy: for instance, as families arrived, they were asked to help dress the altar and arrange the flowers in a vase on the floor. The chapel chairs were used only during the liturgy of the word: at the offertory, the entire congregation gathered around the altar and remained there through the Great Thanksgiving and communion. The music was simple and (during the first weeks at least) very repetitive, to enable non-readers to learn both words and music.

For all the effort to engage children during as much of the liturgy as possible, the planners realistically expected that all the children, but especially the youngest ones, would drift in and out of participation in the course of the hour. Adults, of course, rarely get through a full-length liturgy without significant lapses in attention and participation, but they limit their non-involvement to mild, inconspicuous behavior like staring into space, tapping fingers, or leafing through the bulletin. Children, however, express boredom out loud, and with their whole bodies. Trying to discipline them in church only compounds the problem, adding adult noise and motion to the distraction the kids are already creating.

Even in a setting that they all knew was designed to be meaningful to young children, the parents of St. David's needed help in learning to respond to their children's occasional restlessness not by merely ordering them to be still, or even offering a distraction (a crayon, a cookie, anything to get them to be quiet), but by gently working to re-engage the child with the liturgical action. Quietly pointing out what the priest is doing, priming the child for some familiar words or music about to be said or sung, or simply helping the child to look with wonder at the beauty of stained glass, flowers, or candles, may result in peace and quiet much more effectively than hissing "shhh!" or pinning a child's arms to his sides— and are acts not of discipline, but of evangelism and nurture.

Nonetheless, there will be times when we fail to get our children's attention, and for those occasions there need to be structures in place so that children who are present but not participating can be as undisruptive as possible, and so that it is easy for them to rejoin the worship whenever they are ready. At St. David's, this was done by spreading a rug on the floor to one side of the seating area, with a box of quiet toys (dolls, stuffed animals, books, a few simple puzzles). Most of the toddlers ended up there with their bottles, looking up now and then to see what was going on at the altar, and occasionally commuting back to Mommy and Daddy to check in and be hugged.

The hardest parts of the liturgy to make truly available to all ages are the purely verbal portions. In videotapes made of the first several Services of Celebration at St. David's, there is a noticeable increase in background noise and motion during the lessons and the creed, both of which were merely read, with no attempt to paraphrase, abridge, or dramatize. Mediating the verbal elements of our liturgy to young children without becoming cute or gimmicky is a real challenge, and it was in the homily that the challenge was made most clear.

I was asked to give the homily on the second week of this new liturgy. I had watched the video of the previous week's celebration, and was aware of the drop in focus during the lessons and creed. So I chose to add a visual and tactile dimension to what I said, by bringing in a supply of brightly colored felt symbols and moving them around on a flannelboard as I spoke. The children gathered round and listened eagerly; they all wanted a turn at putting up the flannel symbols; they wanted a say in how they were arranged; they wanted to tell me their ideas and comments and ask me questions. Soon they were clustered so close around the board, and commenting so freely, that their parents, who had remained in their seats, could no longer see or hear what I was doing. Considering the homily to be a "children's lesson," they did not think of coming forward themselves. Instead, they stopped trying to pay attention; eventually, they tuned out completely and began to show their impatience with increasing openness. They fidgeted, they whispered, they shuffled papers. In fact, they *misbehaved*, just as *children* do during the "real" sermon, during Morning Prayer, during anything else they can't follow and know isn't really meant for them anyway. The children and I were so involved with each other that we noticed none of this at the time; when I finished my homily, the kids were still asking for more. But after the service, a woman in the congregation came up to me to say that she hadn't been able to see or hear, and that it was "much too long."

At the eucharist, we are beginning to learn to say to children and adults alike, "Take, eat, this is for you." We have a long way to go before we will have learned how to do the same for the Word. The Word is for all God's children; a "children's homily" that does not say anything to adults does not truly preach the Word. I diminished God's word by gathering only the children to hear what I had to offer; the adults in the congregation accepted and compounded my mistake by not challenging my exclusion of them—by not getting up and coming forward instead of simply tuning out, like children at a boring adult liturgy.

The people of St. David's do not yet have all the answers, but they are learning to ask the right questions: not, "How can we get our children to behave in church?" but "How can we help our children truly to take part in the whole liturgy, word and sacrament, not separately but with us?" and also, "How can we preach the Word so that all can hear it?"

# Chapter 22

# Take, Eat: This is for You

WHEN WE BAPTIZE infants, we are acting out our Hebrew heritage of faith that God's promises are made operative not only by the separate choices of individuals, but also by the corporate choice of the covenant community. The catechism asks, "What is required of us at Baptism?" and replies, "It is required that we renounce Satan, repent of our sins, and accept Jesus as our Lord and Savior." In the case of infant baptism, such a reply is, by the world's standards, sheer moonshine—a fact that the catechism goes on to confront directly. "Why then are infants baptized?" it asks. The answer is that infants are baptized so that they can share in the covenant; promises are made on their behalf by parents and sponsors, "who guarantee that the infants will be brought up within the Church, to know Christ and be able to follow him."

Although we rightly emphasize its celebration within the gathered Body of Christ, baptism is a sacrament of individual faith, individual redemption, individual self-dedication. The candidate or candidates, even if they make up a sizable group, are there as distinct individuals, pointedly called by name, making promises as in-

157

dividuals, washed and sealed and made new as individuals. Yet in this highly personal, individual sacrament we seem to have no trouble accepting the profound theological principle that members of the community may truly act on behalf of each other: promises as sweeping as the vow to renounce Satan and follow Christ may be made by one Christian in the name of another, and be binding, on earth and in heaven.

The eucharist, on the other hand, is quintessentially corporate. Gathered around the altar, we are simply the gathered community. The liturgy nowhere calls on the celebrant to address the communicants by name; all the claims that are made for us, all the blessings that we beg (except in the prayers of the people) are made and asked in the name of us all. If the radically individual, once-only-and-forever blessings of baptism can be received by those incapable of conscious faith, then why not the repeated, day-in-and-day-out blessings of the eucharist? Yet the catechism stops short of even asking such a question.

To the question, "What is required of us when we come to the Eucharist?" the catechism replies, "It is required that we should examine our lives, repent of our sins, and be in love and charity with all people." Period. Perhaps its authors took for granted that the faith, repentance, and charity required as we approach the altar can, like the faith and repentance required at baptism, be graciously attributed to an individual through the corporate faith of the community. But they did not see fit to spell it out. And the omission is a significant one, since, in practice, we clearly do not seem to believe in the adequacy of corporate faith in the corporate sacrament of the altar, though we claim to believe in it in the individual sacrament of the font. After baptizing tiny infants who have not the faintest idea what is being done to them, we then, in most places, exclude them from the corporate meal of the baptized until they "know what they are doing," or "understand what it is all about."

Until twenty years ago, Anglicans considered baptism to be incomplete without the added sacramental rite of confirmation, which provided admission to the eucharist. A certain degree of social maturity and intellectual and spiritual development was required for confirmation, but it was confirmation itself, and not the prerequisites to it, that qualified the individual for communion. Today, on the other hand, we claim that baptism is full initiation and needs no sacramental completion. But we still place intellectual and developmental hurdles between baptized children and the eucharist. The idea of formal communion preparation is so much a part of our inherited tradition that we cannot seem to see how illogical it is in the light of our own professed sacramental theology. It is, moreover, highly questionable pastorally and developmentally.

Our own first daughter, Grace, was baptized at midnight in the Easter Vigil, and slept soundly through the whole experience. No one saw anything remarkable in this, or protested that it made her baptism invalid. But during the years that immediately followed, many people were shocked, amazed, or bemused to see her opening her mouth for the Bread of Life, the Cup of Salvation. When she reached the age at which, in many parishes, she would be "preparing" for her first communion, she had already had six years of the best preparation of all—six years of unfailing confidence that in this place, among these people, in the name of Jesus, she would be accepted and loved and fed, just like everyone else. Infant baptism, followed by six years of exclusion from what is unmistakably the consummation of the Sunday liturgy, would have given her a very different preparation.

People who passionately support the communion of all baptized children are fond of telling anecdotes that show profound intuitions of the significance of the sacrament in children of astonishingly tender age. Many of these accounts are deeply moving. I could tell you a number of them myself, about both my own children and other children I have known and taught. But the very multiplication of these stories, the very need we feel to evince them, betrays how we are still captive to the notion that baptized children must, somehow, prove that they are "qualified" to receive communion—that they somehow "know" or "understand" or "appreciate" that this food is different from an ordinary snack, this gathering from an ordinary party. Many clergy who strongly support infant communion still wait for the child to show she is "ready," by reaching out a hand or asking to be included.

Why? Why do we not then require of infant candidates for baptism that they show signs of "readiness," or prove that they somehow "know" that this water, poured on their head, is different from what happens in the bathtub at home or the plastic pool in the backyard? What are we trying to prove? Does our belief in the Real Presence in the eucharist mean that the eucharist is the only rite we care about enough to establish serious standards for it?

If we began to "believe" in baptism in the same way we "believe" in the eucharist, would we start to be bothered by the idea of its being administered to a four-month-old who is out like a light, or a two-month-old who is screaming his lungs out—or to a baby whose parents have not been to church since their wedding and have bumbled through the vows with no clear idea of what it is all about? Or are we simply more zealous for our Lord's dignity than he is himself? Why do we show such deep resistance to accepting God's gracious invitation, that *all* who have put on Christ in baptism should come and be fed?

If we were not accustomed to it by long habit, we would see in a moment how anomalous it is to insist that children acquire intellectual knowledge of a sacramental act before they are allowed to participate. In our family lives, we express love, forgiveness, and acceptance by hugging and kissing. Hugs and kisses are the sacrament of family love. Every member of our culture knows and understands that touching a baby's cheek with our lips and making a strange little smacking noise signifies our love and care for the baby, and our delight in him. But the baby, at birth, does not know this. He learns, quickly enough, by experience. And we start to teach him to do it too: "Kiss Mommy." "Give Daddy a *big* hug." Kissing and hugging quickly become, for the baby as well, sacramental actions—signs of love and pleasure.

Imagine if, until your child was six, you never kissed her, but only let her watch older people kissing each other. Then, when she had learned to read and write (and, incidentally, had already passed the age where her imagination was most eager to grasp non-verbal experience and make it a part of her deepest self), suppose you sat her down with a special curriculum entitled "Kisses and Hugs: Signs of Love." She would color pictures of people hugging and kissing, and read exemplary stories about families, and answer questions about why we choose this way to express our love. Finally, on a special day, when you were sure she understood enough about hugging and kissing to be truly "ready," you would hug and kiss her for the very first time. She would wear a new party dress, and Grandma would come to lunch and bring a present, and she would feel so proud and so special.

Or would she?

Sacramental actions work directly on our emotions and imaginations; the intellect is only a supplement, important in its turn for full integration of the experience, but secondary in its contribution to our understanding. The early church, intuitively grasping this principle, withheld instruction in the sacraments, even for adults, until *after* they had been experienced. To articulate and codify these emotional and imaginative experiences, and require that the child learn to engage them cognitively, is to deprive them of much of their power. To go still further, and require that the child learn them theoretically before being allowed to experience them at all, is almost to guarantee that they will have only a theoretical power.

In approaching the eucharist with young children, we have tended, understandably enough, to shy away from the sacrament itself and focus instead on liturgy in general. We stress the idea of belonging, of Christian family and community, of sharing food; the shape of the liturgy, the details of words and gestures. In our demythologized culture, these are much more plausible concepts than those at the heart of the eucharistic mystery: creation, sin, alienation; Passover, sacrifice, cross; death, life, flesh, blood.

At best, focusing on "going to church" as we prepare children for communion will leave them free to wonder and speculate about the eucharistic sacrifice, and grow into their own understanding of it. At worst, it will trivialize their understanding and give them a lasting conviction that the powerful mythic language they hear

161

washing over them in church, and the central, ritual action we engage in, are merely traditional forms, and that what the eucharist is really about is nice people coming together on Sunday, like a family, to share a happy but strictly token gift of food and drink.

It's easy enough to explain to children why we come together as a parish family, why we read the lessons and say the creed, confess our sins and pass the peace. It's easy to teach them the right words to say, so that in church they will "know what's going on" and be able to take part, and "understand what they are doing" in that sense. What is just about impossible to explain to a child (or anyone else) is why we do these things with the bread and wine in the first place—what on earth we mean by saying that we are eating the Body and drinking the Blood of Jesus when we pass out little wafers and take little sips of wine.

There is no way to present the eucharist itself in terms that make it intelligible to the discursive mind. We don't really know why a kiss on the cheek feels like love. All the more, we do not know why bread and wine feel like Christ. Psychologists know that even the best "family life" curriculum in the schools cannot possibly make up for a child's own lack of experience of being lavishly, generously loved. Children who have been fed at the Lord's table since earliest infancy are like children who have had plenty of hugs and kisses—they hardly need to be taught about God's love in bread and wine, because they already know all about it; they feel it in their bones. Children who have always been communicants have had years of intuitive engagement with the eucharist through which to build a deep, lasting sense of its meaning—a sense of its meaning that arises from their own experience, their own speculation and wonder about its words, its gestures, its smells and tastes—a sense that is theirs alone. As children grow toward middle childhood and begin to read and write and to desire a more cognitive grasp of all their experiences, then they can be taught *about* the eucharist. Such teaching will be an enrichment of the knowledge they already have, not a substitute for it or a set of adult interpretations that must be grasped before we can trust them with the experience itself.

The image of "first communion" is a hard one to give up—not only because it is simply traditional, but because it strikes deep unconscious chords in us. The experience of union with our Lord through a mysterious physical act is deep and earth-shaking; knowing this, we have a tendency to try to make it special, to "save" it, as it were, until a child is old enough to appreciate it. The Roman Catholic tradition of dressing little girls in white gowns and veils for their first communion has tremendous psychological reverberations. Anglicans have not been so eager to adopt nuptial imagery for first communion, but since confirmation ceased to be the gateway to the eucharist, we have frequently borrowed the imagery of baptism when formally admitting children to communion.

Many parishes make a point of scheduling first communions on the baptismal feasts, or on the Sunday of the bishop's visitation; traditions have been developed involving the use of sponsors, the asking of questions or making of promises, the bestowal of candles or certificates or gifts. The children may come to the altar as a group, singled out from the rest of the congregation, and the course of preparation often climaxes with and individual interview with the rector. All these features work to impart to first communion the sort of solemnity and importance that characterize a transitional or initiatory event. Perhaps the most powerful ingredient of all in our attachment to the idea of first communion is this desire to conform some part of our Christian nurture to the pattern we strongly sense is the true archetype of Christian experience: the pattern of conversion.

Those baptized at a later age, after a period of searching and a momentous choice, will long remember both their baptism and their first communion as truly initiatory moments, as a day when a door was opened at which they had been knocking, and they were at last invited in and welcomed to the family and the feast. That was my own experience, and I know it is wonderful. But in choosing to baptize our children as infants, we have already acknowledged that for them, the pattern of conversion does not apply. It is artificial and futile to use access to the eucharist as a way of imposing that pattern on the Christian nurture of those born in the household of faith—to lock them out of the feast only so that they may have the happy experience of being let in. It remains to us to have the courage of our convictions, and not impugn the dignity of baptism by finding occasions of ersatz initiation for children who have been part of the family all along.

Children raised in Christian families have a different natural pattern, with its own wonders. They share the family's feast as their birthright; they do not have to knock and enter, because they are already home. In Jesus's story that we call the Prodigal Son, the Father has two children. One of them—the one we always seem to notice—"was dead, and is alive again...was lost and is found." But to the other, he says, "Son, you are always with me, and all that I have is yours." Let that be enough.

## Chapter 23

# To Answer for Themselves

AT A CONFERENCE NOT too long ago, a bunch of us Christian education people were standing around telling stories. The conversation came around to the subject of baptism—particularly the baptism of children who are no longer infants. Here is one of the stories:

"We baptized two kids at All Saints'. It wasn't your ordinary baptism. One of the kids, Jimmy, is in foster care; the foster mother is an elderly woman who's very conservative—I guess you could say superstitious. She's uncomfortable unless the kids in her care are baptized, but her own relationship with the church is pretty troubled, pretty uneven. Helen—that's the mom—usually has a houseful of kids, and she brings them all whenever she can get the energy, but she herself is kind of aloof from parish life. We've learned to accommodate all these children—they're great kids, and Helen is very good with them. They're coming more often now, they're more comfortable in Sunday school, and several families in the parish have started to help out with the kids: holding them, chasing them, taking them to the bathroom, and so on. So Helen gets a little peace, and now she's begun to loosen up a bit too.

"We didn't know Jimmy was unbaptized—he's five—and he'd been receiving communion with the rest of the children ever since he first came. He really likes Sunday school, and when Helen got permission from the caseworker to have him baptized, he was very eager for it. She wasn't able to explain to him what it was all about, but she did convey the idea that it was important, and he caught on to that. We kept on giving him communion; we just didn't have the heart to start refusing him. But he certainly knew he lacked something the other kids had, and he knew he wanted it.

"The other boy, Michael, is seven, and a friend of this family. He lives with his grandmother, who is very down on the church. She's devoted to Michael, but there is also an uncle in the household, her youngest son, who can't stand Michael, is always beating on him, and she doesn't do anything to stop it. So Michael spends a lot of time next door at Helen's house with all Helen's kids, and started coming to Sunday school with them. He got very interested in everything that goes on there, and Helen decided that she would try and talk his grandmother into letting him be baptized too. The grandmother agreed, but made no promise that she'd be there to see it happen. Helen is his godmother.

"In a way you could say that both these kids are just looking for something to belong to. But even if that's true, the fact is they were both very sure that they'd found it in the church. They kept asking us how much longer it would be till they could be baptized. So the question was, what kind of pre-baptismal preparation could we realistically do? There was no hope that Michael's grandmother would take part in any such program. Helen was one hundred percent behind the baptisms, but made it quite clear that she was not going to come to any formal preparation: she was much too busy with the kids, and she'd been part of so many baptisms, she knew what it was all about, thank you. Our parish is still working on a written set of standards for baptism, so we really didn't have any norms to apply to coax a little more participation out of Helen, and we decided that was not the place to put our energies. Instead, we would start where we actually were: we'd work with the kids themselves, and treat the Sunday school, rather than the families or the official godparents, as the actual sponsoring community.

"So on the Saturday before All Saints' we had a special Sunday school session. We told stories and made banners about creation, Noah's ark, the Red Sea, Jonah and the whale, Jesus on the cross, and the risen Lord. We cut out pictures from magazines, about water, oil, wind, and fire. We decorated candles for Jimmy and Michael, and gave the kids handbooks we had made with all the words of the baptismal service and a place to write their own names, their godparents' and parents' names, and to draw their own pictures. Using the books, we baptized two Cabbage Patch dolls—boy dolls, not babies. Various kids took the parts of congregation, sponsors, and priest, and Jimmy and Michael spoke for the dolls. They learned the words of the vows, and spoke them loud and clear—especially the ones about renouncing Satan!

"Well, the rector was out of town in the days right before All Saints'. The curate and I had talked it all over; he was supposed to do the baptisms, and he promised me that he would baptize the kids as 'those who are able to answer for themselves.' They would be asked, 'Do you desire to be baptized?' and get to answer 'I do,' and to renounce Satan and profess faith in Christ in their own right. He said we'd also have the sponsors promise to bring the children up in the faith—even though rubrically you don't ask that question if the candidates are speaking for themselves—and that we'd include among those sponsors all the teachers who'd taken part in the day of preparation. The kids would bring their own liturgical handbooks into the service, since that's what they had used when they were learning the vows. And we'd show the congregation all the stuff they'd done during the day of preparation, especially the banners, which were really nice. The rector had a meeting with the vestry before church, so I was supposed to meet the families and godparents an hour before the service and show them what we would be doing in the liturgy.

"So what happened? The next morning the families were late, and by the time they arrived the rector's meeting was over. So when the curate looked for the rector to work out the special aspects of the service, he found him greeting the families at the door, where he completely ignored Jimmy and Michael, and spent the next fifteen minutes going over the service with the only two adults there—Michael's grandmother and Jimmy's godmother, neither of whom had been to church in years, and neither of whom had been expecting to do much more than just be there. Helen was still parking the car and unloading all the other kids. As the procession was forming, the rector informed the curate that he would himself preside over the baptism service through the blessing of the water, though the curate would do the actual baptizing.

"And that's what he did. He looked right through those two kids, who were so eager for baptism, and so eager to answer for themselves. As far as he was concerned, they weren't adults, so they were *infants*. They were standing right there, holding their baptism books, but they never got to say a thing. The rector spoke only to Michael's grandmother and Jimmy's godmother. Those two poor ladies stumbled through the vows, not a word of which they actually believed. Nobody recognized Helen as a sponsor. Nobody called forward the teachers who were supposed to act as additional sponsors. Nobody acknowledged in any way all the preparation the Sunday school had done together. Sure, a lot of that was just a failure of communication in the middle of a frenetic schedule, with the rector's vestry meeting and the families arriving late. But what gets me is, how could he treat those two kids as *invisible?*"

# Chapter 24

# Pages from a Scrapbook

MELISSA, HER PARENTS, and her baby sister Sara were in town from January through the summer during her father's sabbatical from a small southern college. The family were Episcopalians, but had stopped attending church because of some problem with the local parish. During their sabbatical they chose (for reasons I never quite figured out) to enroll Melissa in the local Roman Catholic parochial school. They thought of attending an Episcopal church, but it was one of the things they just hadn't gotten around to.

Melissa was in the second grade. She soon found that her classmates were preparing for a major event in their lives: their first Holy Communion. As one of three non-Roman Catholics in the class, Melissa learned that though she was to participate in all the preparations for this wonderful occasion, she would not be part of the occasion itself. As the day drew nearer, she became increasingly restless, and began to ask her parents to take her to church. At last, on the very morning of her classmates' first communion, Melissa's father brought her to our parish.

It was a festive day in our parish too: the first Sunday with a new rector after a long and painful interim. There was also a baptism. Melissa came to Sunday school, where the day's project was the decoration of a candle to give to the baby's parents. From thin sheets of brightly colored beeswax, the children cut out letters to spell the baby's name, and a host of symbols, some traditional, some fanciful. The beeswax shapes adhere easily to the candle, and look spectacular; Melissa was charmed. She spoke of her baby sister's recent baptism at her grandparents' church, and told us that as a baby she too had been baptized. She said nothing, at that point, of her longing to be admitted to Holy Communion, or of what was going on at that very moment at the parish down the block where she went to school.

Our parish takes very literally the revised rubrics about baptism and communion. Baptized persons of whatever age are welcome at our altar—including, with parents' consent, baptized children of visitors. When newcomers bring their children, I try to find the time to ask whether they are baptized, and to explain that the children are welcome to receive communion from the start: instruction can follow in due course, but the eucharist is the birthright of the baptized child.

I hadn't had the chance to speak with Melissa's father; but when she showed how aware she was of her baptism, I mentioned that she was a member of Christ's body, just as much as the kids who had been coming here for a long time, and that she was welcome to share the bread and the cup with us. I got no particular response, but when we came into church for the baptism, Melissa watched with rapt attention. And when the children and their parents settled down on the rug between the front pew and the altar rail for the Great Thanksgiving, she did not go back to sit with her father, or try to signal him forward to join her. She simply stayed with us, watched everything the priest did, came forward eagerly, held out her hands, and received the Bread of Life. I don't remember that her face was transfigured; I do remember thinking that here was a child who, more than most newcomers, knew exactly what she wanted and where to find it. Only later did I learn the story behind that eagerness.

The following Sunday, Melissa proudly brought her mother and baby sister to church. They attended every week for the three short months until it was time to return home, and at our year's-end festival, Corpus Christi Saturday, Melissa's mother, a sculptor, led the group of children who baked the bread. They made the bread in the shape of a sheaf of wheat, and it was beautiful.

When moving day came, Melissa cried. She said she wished she could hitch our church to the moving truck and take it back to her home town. Her parents left with the resolve to go back to their local parish, even if it did mean working through the troubles they had experienced there. We gave Melissa a communion book when we said goodbye.

David was two. His mother had attended our church briefly some years ago, before she was married, while his father is of the all-too-common type known in this neighborhood as "bummed-out Catholics." (Bummed-out fundamentalists are not unheard of, but in this neck of the woods, bummed-out Catholics are a lot more common.) David's mother, Marilyn, wasn't sure what she believed, but she wanted to be part of a worshiping community, and she chose our parish because she had been there before and it was a compromise between the liberal tradition she thought she would personally prefer, and her husband's Catholic tradition. She came pretty regularly with David, but her husband continued to show no interest at all.

David was unbaptized, and so could not receive communion. Marilyn sat with him on the floor, among the other children and parents, and he wandered around a lot. He never made any trouble; he never made much noise; he just wandered. He would stand at the head of the center aisle and stare intently at the altar. He would drift over to the pulpit, climb up on its bottom step, and climb down again. From the foot of the pulpit, he would stare some more at the altar. Then he'd go back to his mommy.

Marilyn worried that David was being disruptive. I did my best to reassure her: "No, he's not bothering anybody. He is responding, in his own way, to a magnetism he feels from the altar. He knows something special is going on up there. I think you should give serious thought to having him baptized so that he can receive communion."

After a few months, though, Marilyn and David stopped coming. I called her up. She said that the reason was her husband's continuing lack of interest. Concern to accommodate to his heritage was why she had chosen the parish; when he remained indifferent, she switched to the Friends Meeting, where she felt more at home. I asked her, "What about David? He seemed so enchanted by the eucharist, and the Quakers don't have that." Yes, she said, that was true. Quaker meeting wasn't really appropriate for a two-year-old, so David was staying home with his dad on Sundays while she went to meeting.

Amanda is a fifth grader, who came to Sunday school regularly as the guest of one of her schoolmates. She has three brothers and sisters, and they all take part in a dizzying array of activities: ballet, soccer, skating, gymnastics, tennis, swimming team, chorus, the works. Her father has custody of the children, and was pleased that Amanda was coming to Sunday school: "It meant a lot to me when I was her age." He was embarrassed that none of the children had been baptized, and explained apologetically that the family needed to give some serious thought to whether they were ready to participate together in the church—there was some unhappy history to work out here.

The first time Amanda came to church, she was too bashful to come to the altar rail for a blessing. The following week, however, she knelt with her arms crossed, lifting her head under the priest's gentle touch. I thought I saw clearly the longing in her eyes; but then, maybe I was just projecting onto her, since I had spent much of my own childhood with my nose pressed against the glass of the candy store that was the church, wishing that my family would be a part of it. But no, the rector saw it too.

After several months, I met with Amanda's father, and gently (I hope) pressed him on the matter of Amanda's baptism. "Why don't you think about letting her be baptized as an adult? The other children can wait; the whole family does not have to be where Amanda is: the parish can help her take responsibility for her own decision, and support her. I think it would be a wonderful gift to her, and she clearly desires it."

He and the kids talked about it, but we're still at a stalemate. There are still some negative feelings about the church to work out. They don't all feel good enough about it to take on yet another claim on their time, but unlike soccer or ballet, they are unwilling to allow Amanda to take part fully without the rest of the family along. Church is caught in the middle between two images: just one more wholesome activity that a child can go to in a carpool, and a major, whole-family commitment. And Amanda is still kept from the Lord's table, where she longs to be.

Joey and his little sister were baptized last summer. Their aunt was the godmother, and the day when she could be present happened to be one when both the rector and organist were out of town. It was one of those slow Sundays, when five minutes before the service is to begin there is still nobody around and nothing set up. Joey was four. His parents brought him in and introduced themselves to the supply priest and to me. It was the first time they had been to church and the first time I had met them; all their prebaptismal work had been done in private with the rector. I'm not comfortable with that kind of situation—I'd much rather have the family get to know the parish before the children are baptized—but the rector had said there were good reasons, so I concentrated on making Joey feel welcome and at home.

He went to Sunday school for the first half of the service. There, we baptized two dolls: a little boy and a baby. We put water on their heads, and then oil. We had started work on a book of pictures and thoughts about baptism for Joey to take home when his mother came and called us into church. Joey insisted on showing her the dolls and telling her all about the water and the oil. She took the time to listen to him, and then we went in. Perched on his father's hip, Joey looked quizzical as the water trickled down his face. I forgot to look to see if they gave him communion.

At the coffee hour, Joey's mother invited my children and me (my husband was away) to join them for brunch. The food was plentiful and good as family, friends, and neighbors drifted in and out and Joey, my kids, the baby, and several other children made more noise and got dirtier than I would have believed possible. In a brief moment of quiet concentration, Joey sat down to play with his blocks. Rapidly, intensely, he built a church. It had a tall, trian-gular, green steeple at one corner—just like our church.

For the rest of the summer, the family did not come back, but Joey's mother tells me that every time they drove past the church, Joey called out proudly, "That's my church!" In September, they began coming regularly. Six months after his baptism, Joey had a friend staying the night at his house. They were in the bathtub to-gether. Joey poured water on Matthew's head, "in the name of the Father, and the Son, and the Sister."

All these stories are true. I don't quite know what they prove, except what we know already if we give any heed to Jesus' words: that children's spirituality is real, that it matters, that adults and parents and pastors are bound to take it with the utmost serious-ness. For those of us who are called to this ministry, there is noth-ing more thrilling than the gift of being midwife at the birth of faith in a child. And there is a special sadness in watching, help-less, as a child who yearns to be in the Body of Christ and to re-ceive the Body of Christ is kept out.

Children cannot drive themselves to church; they cannot com-pel their parents to bring them; they can't even accept, without their parents' cooperation, the offer of a ride from another family. Children who have wanted to be part of our parish community—

who may have found in it the one place where they were accepted and loved for themselves, the one place where respect was paid to their deepest hopes and fears and longings, the one place where there was beauty, transcendence, and a cycle of stories and rituals that offered meaning and hope—children like these have been withdrawn from the parish by their parents for reasons related entirely to adult agenda. These reasons range from personal spiritual crises to divorce to dissatisfaction with the priest, to burnout from undertaking too many parish tasks, to a schedule conflict with Sunday morning soccer or ice hockey ("We *paid* for that, so he's going to go to it," one parent told me), to an understandable desire to have one morning a week in which everyone in the family can sleep late and then relax together.

It is not the children who resist coming to church—at least, not when the parish program offers children the real gospel rather than the kiddie gospel. When the lessons and worship and art activities plumb the heights and depths of Scripture and the church's year, and the parish reflects the welcoming inclusiveness of Christ's Body—when the church, in short, makes it clear that what it has to offer is faith, hope, and love—then children know they are being fed, and they want to come back for more. We have them, often, for so little time. We can only pray that some of the taste of that Bread of Life, that Cup of Salvation, will stay in their mouths, and, by God's grace, when they are bigger and can make their own choices, they will remember where to find it, and come home.

Part Five

# Good Books

# Chapter 25

# Bibles And Bible
# Stories For Children

T HE USUAL "CHILDREN'S Bible" from American publishers consists of a fairly standard sequence of narratives, told in a vivid and novelistic way, with realistic, almost cinematic, full-color pictures. There are more than a dozen such Bibles for children currently in print, most of them hefty volumes with remarkably similar design, contents and illustration style.

Probably the best of these large-format Bibles is *The Doubleday Illustrated Children's Bible* by Sandol Stoddard (384 pp., Doubleday, 1983), illustrated by Tony Chen. Chen's rather stylized paintings avoid the tired "Bible" clichés, and the book offers a much more inclusive Old Testament canon than most children's Bibles, including selections from the prophets, the psalms, and even the Song of Songs, though the New Testament, as usual, omits the epistles entirely, except to quote brief passages as a supplement to the stories of Paul's ministry.

Also notable are *The Holy Bible for Children*, edited by Allan Hart Jahsmann, with illustrations and maps by Don Kueker (414 pp., Concordia, 1977), an honest and workmanlike attempt to offer an abridged text of the whole Bible (the pictures, unfortunately, are dreadful); and *The Children's Bible in 365 Stories* by Mary Batchelor, illustrated by John Haysom (413 pp., Lion, 1985), which follows the traditional format in every respect, but within the limits of that format, does all of it extremely well.

European publishers are less subject to the ultra-realistic, action-packed visual style, and prefer a more slender, paperbound volume with pictures in a stylized or expressionist mode. A successful example in this style is *A Child's Bible* by a team of British writers and artists, published here by Paulist (288 pp., 1986) and containing a wide selection of stories, tersely and simply told. The narrative, in two-column format, sometimes reads a little like a summary or précis, which may make it less attractive to children. The many small pictures, all in full color, are excellent.

*The Children's Bible* from the Liturgical Press at St. John's Abbey in Collegeville, Minnesota, was originally issued in Germany and has been around since 1959. In 95 pages, it covers in detail only Genesis, Exodus and the gospels, with a brief synopsis of Israel's covenant history to round out the Old Testament. The New Testament ends with Pentecost and a flashback to the parable of the sheep and goats. But within these modest bounds the book is faithful to the content (and often the phraseology) of the scriptural text. The pictures, by Johannes Grüger, alternate page by page between full color and yellow and black only, often resulting in an unattractive dirty olive green for the halftones. An ingenious feature is the table of contents, which not only lists the episodes but briefly interprets them via six simple headings, "Of the good works of God and the evil ways of man," "How God chose the people of Israel as the bearers of salvation," "How God was made man and came to us," and so forth.

*Tomie dePaola's Book of Bible Stories* was published in 1990 by Putnam, and is visually stunning, in dePaola's distinctive, still, hieratic style. The pictures, in soft, rich colors, are reminiscent of early Italian frescoes. DePaola has chosen not to re-tell the stories, but to use carefully chosen selections of the New International Version, arranged on 127 handsomely composed oversized pages. His Old Testament is fuller than the St. John's, including stories from

Judges, Ruth, Daniel, Jonah, and Esther, and a few psalms; his New Testament ends, after the Pentecost story, with I Corinthians 13 and the 148th psalm. The cover illustration and dedication page show the Peaceable Kingdom, leading one to wish fervently that dePaola had used his enormous artistic gifts to give us more such images from the prophets and poetic writings, rather than limiting himself to narratives only.

For very young children—preschoolers and beginning readers—there is a surprisingly successful, and surprisingly complete, volume from Questar Publishers in Sisters, Oregon, called simply *The Beginner's Bible*, with the unfortunate subtitle, "Timeless Children's Stories." It is a compilation from a series of storybooks known as "Dovetales," with pictures by Dennas Davis. The illustrations are on every page, all in full color, in a flat, simple, somewhat whimsical cartoon style: the people are all rather dumpy; the women all have exaggerated eyelashes. But the text is not condescending or cute, and with only half a dozen lines of very large type under each picture, it manages to be quite faithful to the scriptural original in very few words and with very simple syntax. In 520 pages, there is space for some good but fairly obscure stories, such as Balaam, the Gideon cycle, Elijah and Elisha, Josiah and the book of the Law. Probably every single miraculous birth to a childless couple anywhere in Scripture is told in loving detail, which is nice. The compilers refrain at all times from commenting or moralizing on the stories. The only such comment I could find anywhere was at the end of the story of Jesus with the children: "Children are important to Jesus."

Children's Bibles featuring only the New Testament are usually presented as a "Life of Jesus" or an introduction to the person of Jesus. They therefore tend to have a more explicitly spiritual agenda than whole Bibles—to reach out from the text to appeal to the reader's devotional response. The illustrator's image of Jesus, and the narrator's tone, are therefore especially important.

Once again it is the volumes originating in Europe that are most interesting. A particularly striking one is *A Child's Life of Jesus*, with a text apparently developed by a committee, translated from the French by John M. Bomer, and illustrated by Lizzi Napoli (39 pp., Ave Maria Press, 1990; originally published in Paris, 1971). The text, in the present tense, is plain and terse, resembling the gospel narratives themselves (some children may be bothered by the highly inconsistent punctuation, sometimes using quotation marks and sometimes not). The pictures, in luminous opaque tempera washes, are extremely simple and schematic, relying on gesture and composition to convey a mood. The characters are near-silhouettes, with extremely expressive hands, but no faces. A brief historical afterword and list of characters is a helpful feature, though (like so many other writings by Christians about Jews) it describes all Jewish faith, worship, and celebration in the past tense, as though Judaism no longer existed as a living faith.

There are a few volumes now in print that attempt, in various ways, to incorporate for children the whole breadth of Scripture on a liturgical model. Two of them apply some of the principles of the lectionary to the book's organization. *The Macmillan Book of 366 Bible Stories*, retold (originally in Italian) by Roberto Brunelli and translated by Colin Clark, was published in 1988 and runs to nearly 200 pages, with abundant full-color illustrations by Chris Rothero. Both text and pictures come across as competent but a bit bland and wooden: the book has something of a textbook flavor about it, and the stories are often so condensed that they have lost all their vividness. This may be a deliberate device, to send readers back to the original text, whose chapter references are carefully given at the head of each story.

The book is organized by the months of the year, beginning in July; it makes a rapid tour of the Old Testament that ends in mid-December with the messianic visions from Daniel, and gives proportionately more space than most children's Bibles to such themes as the Temple, the Law, the Elijah and Elisha sequence, and the Book of Job. There is biographical material on Isaiah, Jeremiah, and Ezekiel, but almost nothing from their writings, or from the psalms. The gospels are apportioned over the winter and spring, much as they are in the lectionary, with the whole month of April being given to the events of Holy Week through Pentecost. May and June are devoted to Acts, a moral snippet or two from the epistles, and one passage from Revelation.

*Bible Stories for the Church Year*, by Kristen Johnson Ingram with Joseph P. Russell (175 pp., Harper & Row, 1987) is an attempt to organize the Bible for home reading on the foundation of the three-year lectionary. Unfortunately, it is visually uninspired and disappointing in concept. The stories are printed in standard Bible order, first the Old Testament and then the New, with the usual narrative emphasis and the usual distortions and omissions characteristic of children's Bibles. The link with the liturgical year, which is supposed to be the book's selling point, in fact appears only as a series of tables at the end.

A family that followed the editors' recommended schedule of readings would find its attention veering unevenly between the Old and New Testaments week by week (especially in the weeks after Pentecost) and its text sometimes matching one of the week's lessons in church and sometimes not. The editors suggest only one story for each week of the three-year cycle, favoring the gospel reading but turning to the Old Testament in certain seasons and (more confusingly) whenever the lectionary's gospel is deemed unsuitable or uninteresting for children. Texts not in the lectionary are frequently substituted, to supply certain favorite stories that are lacking in the lectionary, or to fill in on days when all the lectionary texts are considered unsatisfactory. The editors make no use of the most salient feature of the lectionary itself: its mutual enrichment of Old and New Testament through the careful provision, for each Sunday, of a Hebrew Scripture, a gospel, an epistle and a psalm.

*Tell Me About Jesus: An Illustrated Prayer Book for Preschool Children*, by Dietmar Brosig, Brunhilde Dinter, and Christel Regenbrecht, translated by Linda M. Maloney and illustrated by Sister Christiane Winkler (Liturgical Press, 1990) is a small hardcover volume of 73 pages originally published, interestingly enough, in East Germany in 1982. The title is misleading; the book actually includes a very brief summary of salvation history, a more extensive tour through the New Testament, a Mass book, and a series of scenes from daily life, concluding, somewhat abruptly, with the statement, "In Advent, we get ready for Jesus to come." (None of the other church seasons are mentioned.) The text is so terse that the parent or teacher will need to flesh it out for the child. The illustrations, in brilliant color, resemble Ethiopian manuscripts and are most effective for the New Testament stories. Small children may be confused by the fact that both the priest in the liturgical section and the family's father in the daily-life section have the same facial features as Jesus. In spite of its eccentricities, the book could be very effective in the hands of a parent or teacher attracted to its style and willing to use it to meditate with the child.

Many Bibles for children are extensively rewritten, in various ways that greatly change the quality of the biblical narratives. When these books are understood to be fiction, they can offer fresh insights, but a child who knows the Bible only through the eyes of one re-teller with a strongly idiosyncratic style, does not know the Bible at all.

*The Book of Adam to Moses*, retold by Lore Segal and illustrated in an austere, sophisticated style by Leonard Baskin (144 pp., Knopf, 1987), provides a spare and haunting narration of the earliest Bible stories, with a distinctively Jewish flavor. At the other end of the literary spectrum, Walter de la Mare's *Stories from the Bible From the Garden of Eden to the Promised Land*, with drawings by the distinguished British illustrator Edward Ardizzone (244 pp., Faber and Faber, 1927, 1977, 1987), enormously expands the stories in a novelistic but formal and rather florid style, interspersed with echoes and quotations from the King James Bible. His account of the Exodus is deeply and beautifully suggestive of the atmosphere of the Great Vigil of Easter, and fills the reader with holy fear.

*Catherine Marshall's Story Bible*, with illustrations by children (197 pp., Avon, 1982) is a composite production. Originally published in Switzerland to showcase work by the pupils of art teacher Michele Kenscoff, it was issued in the U.S. with a new text by the noted religious author Catherine Marshall. Her retellings are highly personal, departing very far from the tone and content of the original Scriptures and frequently adding moral or devotional commentary. The illustrations by the children (group efforts that

sometimes took months or even years to complete) are notable not
for their naiveté or charm but for their elaborate, decorative detail.
A disconcerting feature for the child reader is that armies and soldiers in both Old and New Testaments are usually depicted as
knights in armor, complete with crosses on their tunics and
shields.

Illustrations frequently overshadow the text, as in the case of
*The Bible Story*, with a rather overdone and unremarkable text by
Philip Turner and striking pictures by Brian Wildsmith (142 pp.,
Oxford, 1987). Some children don't like Wildsmith's restless ink
line and extravagant watercolor washes, but for those who do, he
creates some memorable, iconic images. Chief among these is the
image of the City. Looking like some marvelous construction that
children might make with the world's best set of blocks, the City,
like a dream vision, dominates the pictures again and again in
both Old and New Testaments. It's a great shame that Wildsmith's imagination fails him at the end: though the last episode in
the book is a glimpse of Revelation, there is no climactic illustration of the New Jerusalem. Instead, on the last page the City has
shrunk to a Galilean village, with hills and bobbing boats. Rather
than reaching out from the text to touch eternity and our own
lives, Wildsmith has retreated back into "Bible time," and in con-
sequence the whole story seems to withdraw, like the picture on a
TV screen that is sucked into an ever-shrinking circle, then a single
point of light, and finally disappears.

Both author and illustrator may take liberties that not only mis-
represent the Scriptures but pervert them. An egregious example is
*The Crossroad Children's Bible*, retold by Andrew Knowles and illustrated by Bert Bouman (437 pp., Crossroad, 1989, originally
written in Dutch; the American edition is reprinted from a British
translation). This book insults its readers first by the arch and
often silly voice (in the worst style of British writing for children)
with which nearly all the stories are told, including whole episodes
and scenarios that are nowhere found in Scripture, such as this
one, entitled "Abraham Goes Berserk":

It all started with the shop. Abraham's father had a shop that sold gods....On one particular morning, Abraham was doing a roaring trade. And he hated every minute of it! He couldn't believe that these ugly lumps of wood had any power to help anyone. After all, they were only bits of carving knocked up by his father in the backyard....Finally, after the widow from down the road had spent her life's savings on a green monster with four arms, Abraham could stand it no longer. He ran along the shelves knocking all the idols to the floor, and then jumped on them. He felt a lot better straight away!

This elaboration of the story, which changes the atmosphere of Genesis from one of mystery and call to one of near-burlesque, may be based on a Midrash containing many of the same elements (I owe this insight to a friend who teaches Old Testament). If so, it is the more ironic that this volume contains a strong streak of anti-Semitism, rooted in the text and insidiously exaggerated by the illustrator. The pictures, which are stylish and colorful, combine "Bible-style" landscapes, clothes, and artifacts with modern ones in a way that is not only highly confusing throughout, but also sends an extremely offensive message about the Jews.

In the Old Testament the Jews are cast as the good guys: the Babylonian conquerors look like Nazis and the Jewish captives like Holocaust victims. But in the New Testament the tables are turned: the Romans are harmless storybook toy soldiers, while the scribes and Pharisees, against a modern, European, urban landscape, regularly appear as modern Jews. Often they are Hasidic Jews, with exaggerated black hats, side curls, and long noses. While Jesus feasts with the tax collectors and sinners, they are lurking outside, squinting through the window in a sinister way. The low point is reached in a hugely overblown episode where the young Saul of Tarsus is a pupil at Gamaliel's school, and we see him in a bold two-page spread, face to face with some arrogant senior students, who (unlike him) are decked out in full Hasidic style. They quiz him about Jesus of Nazareth, and describe the Nazarene movement with effete and exaggerated horror. "What happened to the rascal?" asks a naive and scandalized Saul. "He's dead and gone," they reply. "Dead and gone. *We saw to that.*" (The italics are mine, but the sentence is climactic, and ends the episode.)

In contrast to the cinematic and sensational style common in single-volume children's Bibles, individual Bible stories in picture-book form are often whimsical, even cute. Concordia's Arch Books are an outstanding example. Some of them are excellent, with texts that are faithful to Scripture, and subtle, suggestive illustration. But often, while the narrative line may be "straight," the re-told text (usually rhymed) and added detail that are the stock-in-trade of such adaptations significantly change the flavor of the story from that of the biblical original.

When a Bible storybook is a retelling of a parable or legend, the originally brief and spare story line must be enormously expanded, simply to bring it up to the size needed to fill the book. A parable is by nature a generic story—like the characters in fairy tales, the people in parables rarely have names, but are simply "the father," "the younger son," "the king," and so on. The events are also generic: people do their daily tasks, are invited to a party; go on journeys or get married or fall among thieves. It is one thing merely to embroider a parable by adding descriptive detail. It is quite another to re-tell it so that the archetypal characters acquire names and character traits and foibles—or to transform it into a modern Aesop's fable, as in Cathedral Films' filmstrip series, *Parables from Nature*, in which the gospel characters are changed into appealing little woodland animals.

Additional vivid details, or varied characters and settings, make the story interesting for children, and fun to watch or read. But they obscure its deeper archetypal shape. For instance, *Parables from Nature*'s version of the Wise and Foolish Virgins is called "The Busy Bee," and teaches the importance of planning ahead...for the coming of winter. Gone is the wedding feast—the joyful anticipation of the bridegroom—the midnight cry, the excitement of bearing the light in a festive procession. The story is profoundly flattened and changed. Similarly, Cathedral's version of the Good Samaritan, "Chuckie Chipmunk," concludes with Chuckie winning the friendship of the squirrel he has helped. The original parable makes no such promise. Combined with the often slick and whimsical style of the illustrations, the effect of such retellings is frequently to lighten up the story, even to burlesque it. Then, as if to compensate, the authors add editorial comment about the meaning of the story, theological or (more often) moralistic.

In another type of Bible story, the additions take over entirely, and a biblical setting or incident is used as the jumping-off point for an essentially fictitious narrative. This technique is widely used in New Testament stories, where it typically serves to bring the reader more closely into the narrative through identification with a child in the story who sees the events at first hand. The character then responds with faith, and the reader is expected to follow suit. The device is an obvious one, a stock-in-trade of Sunday school curriculums, and it can be heavy-handed and coercive.

In the larger format of a novel, however, with an audience of older children, this formula can be enormously powerful. I remember being deeply challenged at twelve or thirteen by Elizabeth George Speare's *The Bronze Bow* (254 pp., Houghton Mifflin, 1961), a Newbery Award winner about a troubled young Jewish boy in the time of Jesus. Daniel's childhood innocence is destroyed by the Romans' crucifixion of his father and uncle, and he nurses his hatred with a band of Zealot outlaws, waiting for the Messiah. Then he meets Jesus, and must make a choice. It had never occurred to me, at twelve, that the choice to trust Jesus and his gospel of love might be hard and ambivalent. I chewed on this story for months.

Bible stories with extensive additions are especially likely to be set in Bethlehem at the birth of Jesus, where they follow a typical pattern: a child or animal who feels lost, sad, or excluded, encounters the baby Jesus and suddenly finds his or her self-esteem restored. Though they may be very appealing to children, nearly all stories of this type are highly suspect theologically. The granddaddy of this genre is *The Littlest Angel*, a theological nightmare that portrays Heaven as a cosmic boarding school where the big, experienced angels snub and humiliate the clumsy, homesick little newcomer, just arrived from earth, and God is the scary, distant headmaster. Not even the surprise ending where the littlest angel is vindicated by God's acceptance of his gift can make up for the horrendous assumptions underlying the story.

Addition of fantasy to the Christmas story is fine, unless it gives the lie to the meaning of the Incarnation. Stories that turn on a dramatic improvement in somebody's life just by encountering baby Jesus, are theologically dubious unless they also (like *Amahl and the Night Visitors*) include doubt and struggle. We want children to know that this baby is a gift to the world, who raises up the lowly and heals our hurts. But he was a human infant, not Superbaby or a newborn demigod with magic powers. He came to us in helplessness and need, and his Messiahship was hidden, revealed only to the eyes of faith—not a kind of incandescent glow that instantly solved problems and changed lives. The challenge to authors and illustrators is to convey both the wonder and the hiddenness of the birth of the Incarnate Lord.

*Christmas in the Barn*, by Margaret Wise Brown with illustrations by Barbara Cooney (Harper Trophy, 1952) is a modest little picture book in the best tradition of early 1950's bookmaking. Brown is unequaled as a prose poet of deceptive simplicity; her text here, like that of her classic *Goodnight Moon*, conveys peace and wonder through slow, resonant vowel sounds and occasional rhyme: "In a big warm barn/ In an ancient field/ The oxen lowed,/ The donkey squealed,/ The horses stomped,/ The cattle sighed,/ And quietly the daylight died/ In the sunset of the west." The Nativity is set, without explanation, in American farm country sometime in the nineteenth century. The setting is pastoral and nostalgic, but at the same time new and strange because it is not the standard robed-and-sandaled "Bible" locale. So though the book radiates peace and beauty, it also challenges even a small child to see the birth of Jesus as miraculous and the Holy Family as travelers in need. The pictures by Barbara Cooney are beautiful beyond praise.

*The First Christmas*, by Robbie Trent with pictures by Marc Simont (Harper Trophy, 1948, 1990) is another small and unassuming volume for young children. This one is simplicity itself, both in text and in illustration style. Each two-page spread introduces a character, setting or event in the Christmas story from Luke: "This is Mary....This is the donkey that Mary rode to Bethlehem....This is Joseph who led the donkey that Mary rode...." There is just enough of the technique of "The House that Jack Built" to delight children as young as two. After the climactic "And this is the baby the shepherds found that first Christmas night in the manger," the very last spread shows all the characters gathered in adoration, with the text of "Away in a Manger."

Much more fantasy appears in *The Donkey's Dream*, by Barbara Helen Berger, with illustrations by the author (Philomel Books, 1985). On the way to Bethlehem, the donkey dreams that he is carrying first a turreted city, then a rocking, shining ship, then a splashing fountain that makes the desert bloom, then a rose, and finally "a lady full of heaven." We watch the unnamed man, lady (visibly pregnant) and donkey arrive at a town and take shelter in a stable. When the child is born, the donkey is led into the stable and the lady says to him, "See what we have carried all this way, you and I"—and the donkey "was not tired anymore, though he had carried a city, a ship, a fountain, a rose, and all the heavens upon his back." As the "Author's Note" explains, all the images in the donkey's dream are traditional types of the Blessed Virgin and have great archetypal power; the text and pictures, however, offer these icons with deft obliqueness, leaving the reader to name the characters and the place and to wonder about the donkey's shining dream.

*A Northern Nativity: Christmas Dreams of a Prairie Boy*, text and pictures by William Kurelek (Tundra Books, 1976) is, in spite of its picture book format, suitable for older children. On the flyleaf appears the simple question: "If it happened here/ as it happened there.../ Who would have seen the miracle?/ Who would have brought gifts?/ Who would have taken Them in?" Set in the Great Depression in Canada, the book shows us the dreams of twelve-year-old William when "the Nativity story got mixed up with his history and geography lessons." He sees the Holy Family traveling with the down-and-out from cowboy camps to Indian villages, fishing towns to ski resorts. Sometimes the Mother and Child are Indians, Eskimos, or Blacks. Often they are turned away; sometimes they are welcomed, even recognized—by children, by members of a rural mission, by others who are themselves down and out. The book's strength is in the concept and in the richly atmospheric paintings, rather than in the text, which is at times obscure, unfocused, or rhetorical. This is a book to pore over, meditatively; it may bear fruit in children's own dreams, and open their eyes to see the face of Christ in the places of their own lives.

Outside the Christmas story, picture books that faithfully convey the mystery and the flavor of the scriptural original, while adding a visual dimension of beauty and depth, are rare indeed, but they do exist. An author-artist we can trust implicitly is Tomie dePaola. One of his best is *The Parables of Jesus* (Holiday House, 1987). Its text is slightly simplified but essentially faithful to the scriptural idiom; the pictures have that combination of glowing color and hieratic dignity we expect from dePaola. Seventeen parables are included, and on the last page, opposite the endpaper, is a full-page drawing of a young monk, holding a candle and looking right out from the book towards the reader, as if to say, with Jesus, "If you have ears to hear, then hear."

*The Parable of the Vineyard*, with text and pictures by Helen Caswell (Abingdon, 1991) sets Jesus' story in a warm and glowing modern location (California, perhaps?) with a kind and mild landowner accompanied by a young child, and successive crews of gentle, peasant-like farmworkers (both sexes, all white). The story is simply and, on the whole, faithfully retold, though one is led to wonder about the significance of the child; Caswell also editorializes on the scriptural original by having the owner say to the disgruntled first work crew, "Was the work so hard? You seemed happy while you were working." It's a shame that authors seem so compelled to add their two cents' worth to their source, especially since Caswell's paintings are lovely, particularly her last image, of a couple and a child (the landowner's family?) with a fiddler and guitarist, dancing under a grape arbor.

Among the most common subjects for Bible picture books are the Genesis stories of the seven days of creation and Noah's ark. Peter Spier has done excellent versions of both, with the profusion of detail that characterizes his style. His *Noah's Ark* (Doubleday, 1977) is delightfully realistic, with its piles of manure, its tumbled bedclothes, baskets full of cats and kittens, and lines of laundry strung across the deck of the ark. But the realism is tempered by images of great simplicity and power: the ark floating alone on the wide waters, by day and night; the dove returning to Noah; the rainbow arching above the newly washed earth.

The Creation story has inspired treatments in all styles, from Spier's realism and detail to the almost completely abstract. A new version of special attractiveness is *Let There Be Light*, with the text of the King James Bible, illustrated by Pauline Baynes (Macmillan, 1990). Her world begins as a static circle; as the seven days progress it burgeons and explodes with life. Plants, stars, fish and birds swarm out of it with increasing speed and multiplicity, until the spread where all the land animals spew forth as from a volcano, and then cascade down the next page with the man and the woman riding the wave of living things like surfers, just released from the hand of God. Finally the creation is once again a circle, or rather a huge oval—brilliant with color and crammed with life, before which Adam and Eve stand in awe. Children who know Baynes' illustrations to C. S. Lewis's stories of Narnia will find particular pleasure in her tribute to God's beauty in our own world.

Two crucial Bible stories for Christians, bracketing the story of salvation, are the fall of humanity and the resurrection of Jesus: "For as in Adam all die, so in Christ shall all be made alive." Though these stories are found in all the Bibles for children, it is rare to find them standing alone, and therefore doubly a cause for rejoicing to find them in superb editions.

Warwick Hutton has adapted and illustrated many of the usual Bible stories for children: Jonah, baby Moses, Noah's ark. But it is in his *Adam and Eve: The Bible Story* (Margaret K. McElderry Books, 1987) that he has found the story that uniquely suits his talent. His illustrations, with a free and delicate line, deepened by light crosshatching and watercolor washes, have a still, sculptural quality that was at odds with the wind and waves in his Jonah and the Great Fish but is superbly right for the mystery of Eden. His God is the simple outline of a robed figure in a radiant halo of white light, solemn and aweful; his Eden is a silent tropical forest with still lakes and huge palms between whose shadowy trunks peep out giraffes, lions and rhinoceroses, their eyes fixing us with stares of deep and inscrutable wisdom. For once in a children's book we see the beasts in all their ancient dignity. Instead of the silly zoo-and-circus animal personalities that are often projected onto the Garden of Eden, or even the innocently joyous exuberance of Peter Spier or Pauline Baynes, Hutton's paradise of the world's infancy is mythic, haunting, and perilous, not charming or carefree. When the human pair takes the fruit, the artist draws back and back from them: we see them from further and further away as we, and they, bid farewell to Eden and to the presence of God who walked in the garden in the cool of the day.

Very different is *Easter: The King James Version* with pictures by Jan Pienkowski (Knopf, 1989). Here, black sihouettes against brightly colored skies convey the violence and drama of the Passion story; the text is studded with illuminated capitals festooned with colored branches—flowers or thorns—on which more silhouettes, tiny ones this time, provide a counterpoint to the story. There is a lamb on one page, a scorpion on another, a cock on the page where Peter denies Jesus; a tiny silhouette of Judas hangs from a branch of Judas tree. As a way of depicting the Passion, Pienkowski's technique is spectacularly effective; it is less so for the Resurrection, where the continued solid blackness of all the silhouettes, including that of the Risen Christ, is disconcerting. The fierce vividness of some of the images, even in silhouette, will disturb some children: there is nothing sentimental or pious about this book, and except for the page with the three crosses against the sky, not a single visual cliché.

These books do not represent a large class of excellent Bible-based volumes for children; they stand out from a crowd of mediocre or boring volumes and a distressingly large number of dreadful ones. We may be grateful that we have them, while praying that there may be more like them, and judging carefully before we put into our children's hands any versions of Bible stories that do not tell the truth—not only in words but in images.

Chapter 26

# Children's Books for the Parish Library

VEN THE SMALLEST parish library would do well to offer other books for children besides Bibles and Bible stories. Not only books about Christian faith, but excellent books on all subjects—particularly fantasy, fiction, and richly suggestive picture books—can stir children's hearts, widen their imaginations, and break down some of the barriers our culture has built between sacred and secular. When a book that makes no claim to be "churchy" or "religious" reveals a world of faith, hope, and love; of humility and courage; of sacrifice, grace, and resurrection; or when it exposes sham and injustice—then we challenge our children to discern in the daily realities of their lives and the private workings of their dreams some of the patterns that are at the heart of the gospel. In so doing, we are helping to give them a foundation of faith and trust, an openness to the hidden working of God in creation, a reserve of moral strength, that is likely to outlast adolescent questioning far better than a mere collection of inspirational stories, doctrinal formulations, and flat-out moral imperatives. As Gail Ramshaw remarks,

Picture books...juxtapose text to image and in a remarkable way evoke primordial images of death and life and enliven our religious imagination....These books are mainly for preschoolers: we must not waste these years. All too soon my daughters came home with Beverly Cleary and Judy Blume, realistic comic light fiction about girls getting through the day. As I believe that what will really get my children through their day, through their life, is a repository of images of life in death, I am grateful...for the foundational images these splendid children's books can give.[1]

The following list, loosely arranged by topic, theme, or genre, is a personal selection of favorites that have stood the test of repeated use, both at home and at church. I have concentrated on picture books for younger children, since they have more flexible uses in parish program; but a few novels are included, for specific reasons. Areas not covered (though a good parish library should certainly feature them) include books on other religious and cultural traditions, and as large a section on biography as the budget can manage. Excellent books are fairly readily available in both these areas. Good books on church history, Christian community, liturgy, celebration and parish life would be nice too, but are virtually nonexistent.

Some of the books on this list are explicitly Christian; most are not. For those who doubt their own ability to determine what makes for literary excellence in children's books, I recommend *Michele Landsberg's Guide to Children's Books* (Penguin, 1985)—especially her incisive discussion of "problem" novels, bibliotherapy, and political correctness (Chapter 10).

## Christian Faith and Spirituality

Baynes, Pauline. *Thanks Be to God: Prayers from Around the World.* Macmillan, 1990.

Books of prayers for children tend toward the overly sweet and radiant—pink-cheeked, golden children kneeling in cosy bedrooms or standing in flower-filled meadows; children from all lands holding hands together, etc. This volume, in both text and pictures, has plenty of beauty and tenderness, but also toughness and strength and a decorative style that is true to the variety of cultures represented. Authors of the prayers range from great saints to contemporary children.

Hodges, Margaret. *Saint George and the Dragon: A Golden Legend Adapted from Edmund Spenser's Faerie Queene.* Illustrated by Trina Schart Hyman. Little, Brown, 1984.

The strength of this book is in the story itself and Trina Schart Hyman's superb illustrations: the adaptation of the text from Spenser's poetry is undistinguished. The legend of the hero who kills the dragon and sets free a captive people is of timeless appeal. Except for the use of "saint" in the hero's name there is no explicit Christian content in the story (in fact there are references to the fairies, which go unexplained); but the pictures are full of suggestive Christian imagery: the cross on St. George's shield; the tree of life that heals the wounded knight; the Holy City on its high peak beyond the end of the world.

Hunkin, Oliver. *Dangerous Journey.* Illustrated by Alan Perry. Eerdmans, 1985.

This adaptation of John Bunyan's *The Pilgrim's Progress* is discussed elsewhere in this book. It has much in common with St. George and the Dragon, while making far more explicit the spiritual meaning of the hero's journey, temptations, struggles and victory. Also available on video, from Gateway Films.

dePaola, Tomie. *The Clown of God.* Illustrated by the author. Harcourt Brace Jovanovich, 1978.

The old legend of the Juggler of Our Lady, in a lovely Italian Renaissance setting. The juggler, grown old and stiff and reduced to begging, enters a church and juggles before the image of the Virgin and Child. Juggling his best, he falls down dead on the floor...but the stern statue of the Child is now smiling. Also available on video, in the Children's Circle series.

Hunt, Angela Elwell. *The Tale of Three Trees*. Illustrated by Tim Jonke. Lion, 1989.

A traditional folktale. Each of the trees has a dream: the first, that it will be made into a treasure chest; the second, to become a great ship; the third, to stand always on the hillside, pointing to heaven. But they are cut down, and the first becomes only a feedbox, the second an ordinary fishing boat, the third merely a pile of beams in a lumberyard. But one day the feedbox holds the Christ Child, and the fishing boat carries Jesus across the Sea of Galilee...and the beams become the Cross. The story is simply and obliquely told, leaving the readers to make the discovery themselves: "And every time people thought of the third tree, they would think of God."

Powers, Mala. *Follow the Year: A Celebration of Family Holidays*. Illustrated by Frances Elizabeth Livens. Harper & Row, 1985.

A miscellany of stories, poems, legends and customs for all seasons of the Christian year. The stories come from all over Europe, with some from the United States or Australia; none from the Third World. All the pictures are of white people, except when the subject of the illustration is brotherly love as an idea. Originally published in England, the book has been Americanized to include Halloween and Thanksgiving, but still carries much of its British flavor: Michaelmas, "Whitsun," and Mothering Sunday (in mid-Lent) are among the holidays featured. Uneven in quality and a little saccharine, the book is nonetheless valuable as a rare attempt to flesh out the church's year for children, including sacred, secular, literary and legendary material on an equal basis, as has often been done for Christmas but rarely for any other feasts.

# Secular or Legendary Christmas Stories

Plume, Ilse. *The Christmas Witch*. Illustrations by the author. Hyperion, 1981.

> An Italian Christmas legend. Befana is an old woman who lives alone. One day she is visited by the Magi on their way to find the Christ Child. They invite her to come with them, but as she hesitates, they move on. She sets off alone, with a sack of toys as a gift to the Child, but she never catches up with the Magi and she never finds the Child. Finally, she begins leaving a toy with every child in the world, in case that child is Jesus. Theologically far more suggestive than the Santa Claus (or even St. Nicholas) story, this legend is also found in Russia, where the old woman is called Babuschka. Plume's illustrations are handsome, though without much distinctive Italian flavor.

Godden, Rumer. *The Story of Holly and Ivy*. Illustrated by Barbara Cooney. Puffin, 1985.

> "This is a story about wishing," begins the narrator. Ivy is an orphan girl in search of the grandmother of her dreams; Holly is a Christmas doll in the window of a toy store. The story of how they find each other and both find a home is intricate and suspenseful, the outcome heartwarming and believable, the narrator's voice always confident and sure, and the pictures, as always when the artist is Barbara Cooney, superb. (The Christian meaning of the holiday is not mentioned.)

Stevenson, James. *The Night After Christmas*. Illustrated by the author. Scholastic, 1981.

> Another story about lonely toys wishing to be adopted by children. A tattered doll and threadbare teddy, discarded by children who received fancy new toys for Christmas, are rescued from the garbage by a gruff old stray dog. They try to

make a new life for themselves in his basement hideout, but succeed only in feeling more and more depressed. The dog's clever plan to find new homes for them is revealed less by the understated text than by the richly atmospheric pictures. Deeply satisfying.

## *Wishes and Dreams, Self-Knowledge, Family Life, Community*

Haas, Irene. *The Maggie B*. Illustrated by the author. Atheneum, 1975.

> Margaret wishes to sail for a day on her very own ship, "with someone nice for company." Her wish comes true, and she manages her little ship, and her baby brother James, with serene self-confidence, even through a storm. The snug, lovingly detailed world of the fantasy ship appeals to children's love of hideouts and playhouses; Margaret's resourceful competence and gentle care for her baby brother are delightful.

Sendak, Maurice. *Where the Wild Things Are*. Illustrated by the author. Harper & Row, 1963.

> A classic that needs no introduction. Max's wish to be as wild as he feels transforms his bedroom into a jungle from which he sails away to where the wild things are. There he tames them and they crown him their king. But after he has had his fill of wildness, he "wanted to be where someone loved him best of all." The supper waiting for him—still hot—is a testimony to unconditional love.

Brown, Margaret Wise. *The Runaway Bunny*. Illustrated by Clement Hurd. Harper Trophy, 1942, 1972.
Lindgren, Barbro. *The Wild Baby*. Adapted from the Swedish by

Jack Prelutsky, illustrated by Eva Eriksson. Greenwillow, 1980, 1981.

>Two more books about unconditional love. No matter how clever the little bunny is at running away from his mother or transforming himself to hide from her, she will always recognize him, always search for him, and always find him. No matter how much mayhem Baby Ben creates, no matter how much he drives his mother to distraction, she never wishes he would just get lost and stay lost: she is always overjoyed when she finds him.

Schenk de Regniers, *Beatrice. Waiting for Mama.* Illustrated by Victoria de Larrea. Clarion, 1984.

>A wonderfully quirky testimony both to the constancy of mother's love and to the power of a child's imagination. Amy promises to wait outside the store on a bench till her mother finishes shopping. She keeps her promise, but worries, "What if I have to wait for a hundred years?" She imagines herself growing up, marrying, having children and grandchildren and dozens of dogs and puppies—still sitting endlessly on the bench. Just as the fantasy threatens to become scary, her mother returns. "Did you get tired waiting? Were you lonely, dear?" she asks. "I got tired waiting, Mama," answers Amy. "But...I wasn't lonely."

Viorst, Judith. *My Mama Says There Aren't Any Zombies, Ghosts, Vampires, Creatures, Demons, Monsters, Fiends, Goblins, or Things.* Illustrated by Kay Chorao. Atheneum, 1973.

>A good book for Halloween. The narrator wants to believe his mother's reassurances, but he keeps remembering times when she has been wrong (many of them humorous). Nonetheless, trust prevails: "Sometimes even mamas make mistakes.... But sometimes they don't."

Leaf, Munro. *The Story of Ferdinand.* Illustrated by Robert Lawson. Puffin, 1977 (originally published by Viking, 1936).
Waber, Bernard. *Ira Sleeps Over.* Illustrated by the author. Scholastic, 1972.

> Two classics about machismo, or the lack of it. Ferdinand is the famous little bull who likes to "sit just quietly and smell the flowers" instead of fighting, even when he finds himself in the bullring by mistake. The narrator and illustrator are masterful as they poke fun at the strutting matadors and the other bulls. Ira is the little boy whose sister shames him into leaving his teddy bear home when he is invited to sleep over at Reggie's house next door. The two boys lie in the dark telling ghost stories with great bravado…till Reggie surreptitiously goes and brings his teddy bear into bed. Ira then feels comfortable about going back home for his. Deftly humorous, especially the portrayal of the obnoxious big sister.

Heine, Helme. *Friends.* Illustrated by the author. Aladdin, 1982.

> Johnny Mouse, Charlie Rooster, and Fat Percy the pig do everything together: adventures, games, sharing food, settling disputes, swearing to be friends forever. At night, when they have to separate because they do not fit in each other's houses, they dream about each other, as good friends do. Joyous, witty and unsentimental.

Zolotow, Charlotte. *I Know a Lady.* Illustrated by James Stevenson. Puffin, 1984.

> A very simple tribute, narrated by a little girl, to the solitary old lady on the block who bakes treats for children, gives them flowers, pats their dogs and knows their names. "I wonder what she was like when she was a little girl. I wonder if some old lady she knew had a garden and cooked and smiled and patted dogs and fed the cats and knew her name." The narrator concludes by imagining herself as an

old lady, and the old lady as a little girl, and feels sure that "I would love her a lot, the way I do now."

Lobel, Arnold. *Uncle Elephant.* Illustrated by the author. Harper & Row (an I Can Read Book), 1981.

Lobel is a master at telling substantial stories in very simple vocabulary and syntax: his Frog and Toad series are wonderfully warm and humorous. Uncle Elephant, however, is in a class by itself. It begins like true fairy tales, with a catastrophic loss: the narrator, a little elephant, is sitting alone in his room with the curtains closed because his parents have been lost at sea. His Uncle Elephant opens the door. "Now come out of this dark place," he says. There begins a touching friendship between the old and wrinkled uncle and the young nephew, who is both sad and brave. They play together, comfort each other, and bond deeply to each other. When the nephew's parents are rescued and return to claim him, the joyous reunion is tempered with a new sadness, for the end of a special time together.

Rylant, Cynthia. *The Relatives Came.* Illustrated by Stephen Gammell. Bradbury Press (Macmillan), 1985.

A superb marriage of text and pictures, portraying an improbably numerous and eccentric batch of relatives, piling into their old jalopy, driving all day, and descending in droves on the narrator's family. "You'd have to go through at least four different hugs to get from the kitchen to the front room." The pictures are full of crazy, funny details as well as genuine affection and zest for simple daily pleasures.

# *Natural Order, Life Cycle, Change, Loss and Death*

Azarian, Mary. *The Tale of John Barleycorn or From Barley to Beer.*
Illustrated with woodcuts by the author. David R. Godine, 1982.
> This is the book we use in celebrating Corpus Christi. John
> Barleycorn, the personification of the grain, dies and rises
> again to give life to the community; the people, who have
> buried him, cut him down, tortured, racked and beaten him,
> are astonished that he "lived to tell the tale," and in passing
> the jug they celebrate the work of their hands and the sacrifi-
> cial goodness of creation. Subtly and profoundly eucharistic.

Hall, Donald. *Ox-Cart Man.* Illustrated by Barbara Cooney. Puffin, 1979.
> A lyrical evocation of the seasons in nineteenth-century New
> England, where the peddlar and his family live frugally
> throughout the year, planting, harvesting, shearing sheep,
> and fashioning whatever is left over from their own immedi-
> ate needs into goods for the father to trade at Portsmouth
> market in the fall. A Caldecott Medal winner.

Williams, Margery. *The Velveteen Rabbit or How Toys Become Real.*
Available in various editions, with various illustrators. Date of
original publication not given.
> The classic story of the little stuffed rabbit who becomes
> "real" because a child has loved him and played with him—
> "By the time you are Real, most of your hair has been loved
> off, and your eyes drop out and you get loose in the joints
> and very shabby. But these things don't matter at all, because
> once you are real you can't be ugly, except to people who
> don't understand." Finally, the rabbit must be disposed of,
> because the boy has played with him while sick with scarlet
> fever; the Nursery Magic Fairy endows him with new and

truly "real" life. Very British, and dated in style and tone, but perennially well-loved. Also available on video, and on audio cassette in several different versions.

dePaola, Tomie. *Nana Upstairs and Nana Downstairs*. Illustrated by the author. Puffin, 1973.

Four-year-old Tommy loves his grandmother (Nana Downstairs) and his great-grandmother (Nana Upstairs) who is 94 and bedridden. He has a special friendship with Nana Upstairs, who gives him candy and shares secrets with him. On the night after her death, he sees a shooting star. His mother tells him, "Perhaps that was a kiss from Nana Upstairs." Later, when Tommy has grown up, Nana Downstairs also grows old and weak and eventually dies. Seeing another shooting star, Tommy thinks, "Now you are both Nana Upstairs." The memories of childhood are tender and precise; the presentation of death, while lacking any specifically Christian dimensions, hints at the transcendent power of memory and love.

Douglas, Eileen. *Rachel and the Upside-Down Heart: A True Story*. Illustrated by Katherine Potter. Price, Stern, Sloan, 1990.

When Rachel is four, her father dies, and she leaves her pretty house in Kentucky and comes to live in New York City. For a while she is so sad that whenever she draws a heart, she draws it upside down; but gradually, as she finds friends and interests, she learns to be happy again, and then to reach out to a friend whose father has died. Emotionally true, but with (in passing) some dicey theological formulations, such as, "Daddy got broken, [Mommy] explained. He couldn't be fixed. Not here, anyway. He had to go to a place called heaven." This choice of words implies that heaven is a place of exile, even of punishment. No mention of God— only of heaven, and Daddy looking down on Rachel from heaven.

Sanford, Doris. *It Must Hurt a Lot*. Illustrated by Graci Evans. Multnomah Press, 1986.

A very simple story about the death of a boy's puppy, tenderly hand-lettered on pages bordered by warmly colored quilt squares. The second half of the book offers the reader a series of "secrets," summarized from the painful episodes in the first half: "When I love lots I hurt lots;" "My friends want to help; they just don't know how;" and so on. The intimate tone established by the narrator saves this part from becoming condescendingly therapeutic. In the last spread, we see on the boy's bedroom wall a framed picture of the Good Shepherd; and the endpapers offer both a list of suggestions for adults to help children deal with loss, and an address to write to for "information" about God and heaven. (This title is the best in the "Heart to Heart" series, others of which deal with divorce, sexual abuse, etc.)

Alex, Marlee and Ben. *Grandpa and Me: We Learn About Death*. Illustrated with photographs by Ben Alex and Otto Wikkelsoe. Bethany House, 1982 (originally published in Denmark, 1981).

An explicitly Christian exploration of death, beginning with a happy springtime visit by six-year-old Maria to her grandparents' farm. The animals' cycle of birth and death, the seeds for this year's flower garden, bedtime prayers, and reading the Easter story in the Bible, combine to introduce Maria to both natural and theological dimensions of life and death. Some weeks later, at home in the city, she learns that her Grandpa is very sick. She visits him in the hospital and says goodbye; a few days later, he dies. At her next visit to the farm, Maria and her grandmother cry together, and Grandma describes Grandpa's funeral in terms that are full of Christian hope.

# Folk Tales, Fairy Tales, Fantasy

McDermott, Gerald. *Arrow to the Sun: A Pueblo Indian Tale.* Illustrated by the author. Puffin, 1977 (Viking, 1974).

A Native American legend with striking similarities to the story of Jesus' incarnation and resurrection. Illustrated in hot colors and vivid geometric shapes modeled on Southwestern Indian folk patterns.

dePaola, Tomie. *The Legend of the Bluebonnet: An Old Tale of Texas.* Illustrated by the author. Putnam, 1983.

Stricken by a drought, the Comanche people pray to the Great Spirits for guidance. The shaman tells them that the earth will be restored only when the people have sacrificed their most valued possession. No one is willing to make such a sacrifice except a young girl called She-Who-Is-Alone, who climbs the holy mountain alone and offers her warrior doll, the only keepsake she has from her dead parents. When she awakens in the morning, the rains are returning, and the earth is covered with blue flowers the color of the feathers on the doll's headdress. And the people give her a new name: One-Who-Dearly-Loved-Her-People.

Mayer, Mercer. *East of the Sun and West of the Moon.* Illustrated by the author. Aladdin, 1980.
Mayer, Marianna. *Beauty and the Beast.* Illustrated by Mercer Mayer. Aladdin, 1978.

Two superb fairy tales, superbly illustrated by Mercer Mayer (who is better known for his series of whimsical "Little Critters" stories). Both are filled with haunting beauty, brooding fear, sudden reversals, severe trials, love, constancy, and hope. In both stories, it is the gallant (though fallible) maiden who rescues and sets free the enchanted prince.

de Brunhoff, Jean. *The Story of Babar, the Little Elephant.* Translated from the French by Merle S. Haas. Illustrated by the author. Random House, 1933.

> A modern classic, with an archetypal fairy-tale plot: the catastrophic loss of a loving mother, the young hero's journey into the world to seek his fortune, his acquisition of civilized skills and graces with the help of a generous mentor, and his triumphant return to his original home to share blessings with the community, claim his bride, and be crowned king. With no heavy-handed hidden meanings, it is still the story of achieving maturity: mastery over one's own animal nature and mastery of sorrow at the loss of paradisal babyhood.

Steig, William. *Sylvester and the Magic Pebble.* Illustrated by the author. Simon & Schuster, 1969.

> One of Steig's best, though all his many books (*Brave Irene, The Magic Bone, Spinky Sulks, Caleb and Kate, Doctor de Soto, Abel's Island,* and more) are superb. A story of magic gone out of control because of the young hero's careless haste...and a benevolent universe that finally restores him to his heartbroken parents.

Lamorisse, Albert. *The Red Balloon.* Illustrated with photographs from the film, *The Red Balloon.* Doubleday, 1956.

> A lonely young Parisian boy named Pascal is befriended by a magic balloon with a mind of its own. But his wonderful possession arouses the jealousy of a gang of older boys, who chase him, corner him, and out of sheer spite, destroy the balloon. As Pascal sits crying on the ground, hundreds of other balloons materialize from all over Paris and cluster around Pascal: in the final scene we see him riding a huge bunch of balloons, high over the roofs of the city. A rich and strange transformation (conscious or not) of the gospel story. Also available (the original movie) on video.

# *Fiction*

There are hundreds of excellent novels for children from eight to fifteen or so. If in doubt, start with the Newbery medalists; also acquire the habit of reading children's novels yourself. Many of them are every bit as well written as the best contemporary literature for adults. There is room to cite only a very few novels here—a handful of stories that (without compromising their integrity as imaginative fiction) venture to engage theological issues, or to portray believable children struggling with issues of faith. There is a huge number of good stories in which children struggle with their own self-understanding, with issues of moral choice, with their role in society and the passing of childhood. But explicit concern with Christian theological formulations, and explicit mention of membership in a Christian community (other than passing references to "going to church,") are almost unheard of. Some of the books listed here do break that taboo; the last two may perhaps even signal the beginning of a trend.

Lewis, C.S. *The Lion, the Witch and the Wardrobe* and other
Chronicles of Narnia. Illustrated by Pauline Baynes. Macmillan,
1950-1957.

> Absolutely the classic stories for children, beloved by virtually all their readers whether they pick up on the Christian themes or not (I do know one intelligent Jewish child who realized partway through the series that there were Christian meanings behind the characters and plots, and refused to read on). The stories are not "allegory" in the sense that they were written to be decoded into exact equivalents of the Gospel. They are fantasies: imaginative responses to the totally open-ended question, "How might our God have acted in another world?" Even if the stories are used in Christian education, it would be best to leave children to discover meanings for themselves, rather than try to elicit particular interpretations. Film versions are also available, but are very poor substitutes for the books: the robotic Aslan, chubby and

bucktoothed Lucy, and Hollywood-sexy fauns and nymphs are among the many jarring elements in the BBC film versions; the American-made animated version is skimpy and technically poor.

L'Engle, Madeleine. *A Wrinkle in Time.* Dell Yearling (Farrar, Straus & Giroux), 1962.

Almost as classic as the Narnia books, L'Engle's "Time" series explores issues of calling, quest, and spiritual gifts as well as the fantasy question of how God might act in other worlds. The later volumes become mannered and precious, but *A Wrinkle in Time* still has a great deal of freshness and originality, and even on the twentieth rereading, the climax where Meg rescues Charles Wallace simply by the power of loving him brings tears to the eyes.

Speare, Elizabeth George. *The Bronze Bow.* Houghton Mifflin, 1961.

Described with children's Bibles and Bible stories in the previous chapter, this book stands alone in its forthright depiction of a troubled and angry Jewish boy in the time of Jesus, struggling to find the strength to believe and forgive.

Babbitt, Natalie. *Tuck Everlasting.* Farrar, Straus, and Giroux, 1975.

A tersely written, extraordinarily subtle tale about what happens when a family finds a magic spring that imparts eternal youth. What would it be like to be exempt from death? Natalie Babbitt's novels touch obliquely on the supernatural — belief, superstition, communal myths and rituals — and delicately pose deep metaphysical questions.

Paterson, Katherine. *Bridge to Terabithia.* Illustrated by Donna Diamond. Harper Trophy, 1977.

The story of a friendship between two lonely fifth-graders in a West Virginia town — Jess, a sensitive mountain boy who loves to draw, and Leslie, transplanted from Washington D.C. by her "back-to-the-land" parents — and the magical world they create together. Christian faith enters obliquely — Leslie, the liberally brought up free-thinker, accompanies Jess's family to church on Easter and sees power in the story that is lost to them in their preoccupation with the social details of churchgoing. But the story is mostly about Leslie's tragic death and the way it challenges Jess to grow up and to learn to love. Sensitively written, though with some regional and class stereotypes.

Blume, Judy. *Are You There, God? It's Me, Margaret.* Dell (Laurel Leaf), 1970.

Blume, one of the most popular of contemporary children's authors, can be glib, shallow, and exploitative, especially as she deliberately sets out to break taboos. However, in her assault on the taboo against religion in children's fiction, she doesn't do too badly. Her Margaret is an appealing if confused twelve-year-old who is struggling to complete a school assignment about religious faith in a mixed Jewish-Gentile family where none of the adults want to deal with her questions.

Rylant, Cynthia. *A Fine White Dust.* Dell Yearling, 1986.

Strikingly original and well-written novel about a young boy, powerfully attracted to the church since early childhood despite his parents' benign indifference. Pete falls under the spell of an itinerant revival preacher, and prepares to leave father and mother and all that he has. But the preacher stands him up, and he must struggle with the discord between who talks Christian in his life and who he can really count on to stick by him — and he must figure out where God fits in all this. Groundbreaking writing for young people.

Cormier, Robert. ,*Other Bells for Us to Ring*. Illustrated by Deborah Kogan Ray. Delacorte Press, 1990.

Darcy has never had a best friend, because she and her parents never stay long enough in one place. But during World War II, while her father is in the service, she makes friends with Kathleen Mary O'Hara, who wears her Catholicism like a badge and even sprinkles Darcy with holy water and tells her that now she is a Catholic too. Struggling with loneliness and then with unexpected loss and dismay, Darcy finally seeks help from an aged nun with a reputation for sanctity, and finds, if not a miracle, nonetheless a measure of peace and the strength to go on living.

# NOTES

1. Gail Ramshaw, *Worship: Searching for Language* (Pastoral Press, 1988), pp. 35-36.

# Chapter 27

# Understanding
# Children's Spirituality

T HE STUDY OF CHILDREN'S spirituality is a small but highly fragmented field. People find their way into it from a wide variety of disciplines—social anthropology, clinical and developmental psychology, religious education, pastoral theology, liturgics—and often seem to be unaware of work that has been done in the area by those outside their own academic subculture. The following list is not a comprehensive bibliography of the field, nor a list of every work cited in this book, but a selection of books, from many different viewpoints, that reveal our calling to open the whole of God's Word—and to preach an undistorted Gospel—to ourselves and our children.

A basic knowledge of the Scriptures is, of course, indispensable for Christian parents and teachers. There are many excellent historical and critical introductions to the Bible available for adults, but this list does not attempt to include them. For a focus on the scriptural narrative as story and mystery, try the many theological books by Robert Farrar Capon, especially *Hunting the Divine Fox* (Seabury, 1974). Capon is the only modern writer I know to give the images of Jerusalem and the Bride and Bridegroom the same value they have in historic catholic liturgy and spirituality.

Most of the books included on this list are in print as of this writing. Those that are not should be available from a reasonably well-stocked church resource center.

Apostolos-Cappadona, Diane. *The Sacred Play of Children*. 148 pp. Seabury, 1983.

Excellent collection of essays from Roman Catholic, Protestant, and Eastern Orthodox perspectives, with theological, psychological and developmental insights into the meaning of faith and worship for children, appropriate content for children's liturgies, and implications of the presence of children for the parish community.

Berryman, Jerome. *Godly Play: A Way of Religious Education*. 172 pp. Harper San Francisco, 1991.

Theoretical framework for Berryman's work with children since his encounter with Sofia Cavalletti. The book is primarily speculative and densely anecdotal (including much autobiography, historical excursions ranging from Socrates to Van Gogh, and references to a host of modern thinkers); the central chapters describe Berryman's actual teaching techniques in considerable detail.

Bettelheim, Bruno. *The Uses of Enchantment: The Meaning and Importance of Fairy Tales*. 328 pp. Knopf, 1976 (paper: Vintage, 1977).

Seminal exploration of the role of fantasy and story (especially traditional stories in which the hero prevails and the evil are punished) in children's emotional lives, and the importance of giving children the space and the freedom to work out their own interpretations of stories, without adult explication or moralizing. Detailed exploration of several traditional stories, in orthodox Freudian terms. Bettelheim is not interested in the New Testament and does not apply his own model to the biblical story; the possibilities, however, are extremely rich.

Cavalletti, Sofia. *The Religious Potential of the Child.* Translated from the Italian by Patricia M. Coulter and Julie M. Coulter. 187 pp. + 50 pp. of plates. Paulist Press, 1983.

A challenging theology of children's spirituality, based on the conviction that all children have an intuitive knowledge of God; the job of the teacher and worship leader is to provide the stories and the vocabulary to enable the child to articulate and name that experience and find a place in the worshiping community. General description of Cavalletti's Montessori-based method of instruction and worship with children. Many samples of children's drawings; some photographs of children at worship in classrooms and chapels. Roman Catholic orientation but most points are applicable to all liturgical denominations. For how-to-do-it, see Stewart and Berryman, below.

Coles, Robert. *The Spiritual Life of Children.* 351 pp. Houghton Mifflin, 1990.

Reports of interviews conducted throughout Coles' forty-year career studying children in a wide variety of cultural and social settings. Anecdotal and tantalizing; Coles concentrates on the most fascinating and articulate children, who display some astonishing insights and reveal vivid inner worlds. The questions that preoccupy them—God and nature, God and evil, heaven and hell, sincerity and hypocrisy, God and the self—are the same as those revealed in Robinson's *The Original Vision*, and are quite different from the content of most Sunday School curriculums.

Fowler, James W. *Stages of Faith: The Psychology of Human Develop-ment and the Quest for Meaning.* 305pp. + appendices and index. Harper & Row, 1981.

> Classic scholarly exposition of developmental stages in the growth of human capacity to trust, to find meaning in life, and to make commitments. Draws on Piaget, Erikson, Kohl-berg, as well as Freud, Bettelheim and many others.

Gobbel, A. Roger and Gertrude G. *The Bible: A Child's Play-ground.* 160 pp. Fortress, 1986.

> Developmentally-based argument for allowing children to meet the Bible on their own terms, without fear that they will "misunderstand" it unless adults supply "correct" interpreta-tions. The authors argue that children are more likely to achieve mature, theologically sophisticated understandings if they have experienced a wide range of Bible stories without prescribed interpretation, and that reducing a story to a par-ticular "meaning" or "lesson" carries the risk of children's getting "stuck" at that level of interpretation because the teacher endorsed it. Strongly critical of most "Bible stories" for children.

Gray, David and Elizabeth Dodson. *Children of Joy: Raising Your Own Home-Grown Christians.* 247 pp. + bibliography of suggested children's books (now seriously out of date). Roundtable Press (4 Linden Sq., Wellesley, MA 02181); published 1975 but written in mid-1960s.

> Excellent, detailed suggestions for celebrating daily life, the story of salvation, and the seasonal round with preschool and school-age children. Plenty of serious discussion of theologi-cal issues—this is not (unlike many books on family celebra-tion) primarily a craft book that will give the family the feeling that they ought to be spending all their time cooking, cutting, and pasting together. Emphasis on choosing stories, books and songs. Dated in many ways, but still very useful.

Halmo, Joan. *Celebrating the Church Year with Young Children.*
127 pp. (large format, illustrated) + appendices, including musical
selections and bibliography. Liturgical Press, 1988.

> Extremely complete guide to family liturgical celebration with
> preschool children, at home and in the context of (Roman
> Catholic) parish community. Heavily influenced by Cavalletti
> movement. Presents Sunday as "the weekly Pasch," then the
> Paschal season and Lent, then Christmas and Advent. Abun-
> dant simple crafts and recipes, suitable for Sunday School as
> well as home use; also numerous low-tech ideas (things to no-
> tice and talk about at different seasons, for example). Very
> different approach from the verbal-theological emphasis of
> *Children of Joy.* Illustrations include many drawings by chil-
> dren. (See also Nelson, *To Dance With God,* below.)

Hanchey, Howard. *Creative Christian Education: Teaching the Bible
through the Church Year.* 185 pp. Morehouse, 1986.

> In this and a later companion volume (*Christian Education
> Made Easy*), Hanchey sketches the structure of educational
> program with infectious enthusiasm and a multitude of excel-
> lent practical tips. Principal points include the liturgical year
> as syllabus and the desirability of homegrown rather than
> purchased curriculums. Discussion of program's theological
> content remains somewhat sketchy. Emphasis is on "suc-
> cess," and on having "fun" with education; elements of tran-
> scendence and mystery are somewhat underrepresented.

Nelson, Gertrud Mueller. *To Dance With God: Family Ritual and
Community Celebration.* 245 pp., illustrated by the author. Paulist
Press, 1986.

> An excellent complement to *Children of Joy,* balancing its ver-
> bal focus (and its view of the family as an isolated and inde-
> pendent Christian community) with an emphasis on the
> social and psychological implications of celebrating the mys-
> teries of faith in community—both the family community and

216

the parish community. Handsomely designed and illustrated, representing an eclectic brand of American Roman Catholicism (Northern European, Hispanic, and Native American traditions predominate), with much homage paid to Carl Jung. Some craft and recipe suggestions, but the main emphasis is on enacted ritual and family and parish traditions. Designed for use by families with children of all ages, through adolescence (in contrast to preschool focus of *Celebrating the Church Year with Young Children*).

Ng, David, and Virginia Thomas. *Children in the Worshiping Community.* 156 pp. John Knox Press, 1981.
Excellent all-round discussion arguing for full participation of children in mainstream congregational worship and parish life. Sympathetic insights into experience of Sunday worship from child's-eye view; specific suggestions for program; discussion of children's choirs and children's sermons. Presbyterian perspective; very little material on sacraments.

Ramshaw, Gail. *Worship: Searching for Language.* 213 pp. Pastoral Press, 1988.
A collection of essays by one of the most interesting writers on language and liturgy today, many of which show special insights into the power of stories for children, and the need to revive some ancient ways of looking at Scripture and liturgy.

Robinson, Edward. *The Original Vision.* 171 pp. Seabury, 1983 (first published 1977, in England).
A report on a voluntary study of adult spiritual experience, which revealed a surprising prevalence of intense religious experience in childhood and a marked similarity in the quality of that experience—usually springing from an encounter with nature, light, or music, and characterized by powerful intui-

tions of goodness, harmony, mystery, and love. Implicit critique of many of the ways we present faith to children.

Russell, Joseph P. *Sharing Our Biblical Story: A Guide to Using Liturgical Readings as the Core of Church and Family Education.* 329 pp. Morehouse, 1979, 1988.

Recent reissue, with revisions, of a highly influential guide to understanding the lectionary as the church's basic syllabus, with detailed practical suggestions for centering parish education on lectionary and liturgy. Chapters include: "The Religious Educator as Storyteller," "An Overview of the Historical, Literary, and Theological Development of the Bible," "Sharing Our Story in the Liturgy (Liturgy as Dramatization)," model programs for lectionary-based seasonal educational programs, and detailed commentaries, with program suggestions, on all three years of the Sunday lectionary, plus the saints' days and other holy days, a new section on the Common Lectionary, and a lengthy annotated bibliography.

Stewart, Sonja M., and Jerome W. Berryman. *Young Children and Worship.* 214 + 120 pp. of patterns for wood figures and other materials. Westminster/ John Knox, 1989.

Detailed how-to book for an American adaptation of the Cavalletti method, developed by an Episcopalian and a Presbyterian, with brief introductory chapters giving theological and developmental rationale.

Stewart, Stan, with Pauline Stewart and Richard Green. *Going to Church with Children.* 119 pp. Melbourne, Australia: Joint Board of Christian Education, 1987.

Useful book aimed mainly at parents, arguing for full participation of children in mainstream parish worship. Many practical helps and encouraging perspectives; advice on managing conflict within the parish between those who want children in church and those who do not. Suggests that parents encourage children's participation in worship by teaching traditional hymns at home and playing taped organ music at rest time so as to associate "church" atmosphere with quiet, comfort, and peace.

Westerhoff, John H. III, and William H. Willimon. *Liturgy and Learning through the Life Cycle.* 182 pp. Seabury, 1980.

This is just one of many books by two of the most prolific writers on Christian nurture, liturgy, and pastoral theology today. It provides theory and practical suggestions for incorporating spiritual and personal growth of both individuals and families into the parish liturgy and argues strongly for use of the church year as primary curriculum and inclusion of children in all parish celebrations.

COWLEY PUBLICATIONS is a ministry of the Society of St. John the Evangelist, a religious community for men in the Episcopal Church. Emerging from the Society's tradition of prayer, theological reflection, and diversity of mission, the press is centered in the rich heritage of the Anglican Communion.

Cowley Publications seeks to provide books, audio cassettes, and other resources for the ongoing theological exploration and spiritual development of the Episcopal Church and others in the body of Christ. To this end, it is dedicated to developing a new generation of theological writers, encouraging them to produce timely, creative, and stimulating publications of excellence, and making these publications available widely, reaching both clergy and lay persons.